8 Steps to CLASSROOM MANAGEMENT SUCCESS

This book is dedicated to teachers, school counselors, members of child study teams, school administrators, and all other education professionals who tirelessly work, often in the face of substantial obstacles, to educate our students.

8 Steps to **CLASSROOM MANAGEMENT SUCCESS**

A Guide for **Teachers** of **Challenging Students**

GEORGE KAPALKA

CORWIN
A SAGE Company

For information:

Corwin
A SAGE Company
2455 Teller Road
Thousand Oaks, California 91320
(800) 233-9936
Fax: (800) 417-2466
www.corwinpress.com

SAGE Ltd.
1 Oliver's Yard
55 City Road
London EC1Y 1SP
United Kingdom

SAGE Pvt. Ltd.
B 1/I 1 Mohan Cooperative
   Industrial Area
Mathura Road, New Delhi 110 044
India

SAGE Asia-Pacific Pte. Ltd.
33 Pekin Street #02-01
Far East Square
Singapore 048763

Printed in the United States of America

Library of Congress Cataloging-in-Publication Data

Kapalka, George M.
8 steps to classroom management success: a guide for teachers of challenging students/George Kapalka.
    p. cm.
Includes bibliographical references.
ISBN 978-1-4129-6943-7 (cloth)
ISBN 978-1-4129-6944-4 (pbk.)
    1. Classroom management. 2. Problem children—Behavior modification.
I. Title. II. Title: Eight steps to classroom management success.

LB3013.K325 2009
371.102′4—dc22   2008056018

This book is printed on acid-free paper.

09   10   11   12   13   10   9   8   7   6   5   4   3   2   1

Acquisitions Editor:	Jessica Allan
Editorial Assistant:	Joanna Coelho
Production Editor:	Veronica Stapleton
Copy Editor:	Tina Hardy
Typesetter:	C&M Digitals (P) Ltd.
Proofreader:	Dennis W. Webb
Cover Designer:	Michael Dubowe

Contents

Foreword

For over 25 years, a large part of my work as a school psychologist has been dedicated to discovering the root causes of pathological behavior in children and devising effective interventions to treat them. As s neuropsychologist in school, private practice, and hospital settings, I have found that one of the most pressing questions universally encountered by teachers and mental health professionals alike is this: "How can we positively and effectively influence the behavior of our most troubled children *and* motivate them to exhibit this improved behavior in a consistent, appropriately generalized fashion?"

Often, research literature in the fields of education and psychology is weighted too heavily toward the theoretical. A large proportion of published material in these intertwining disciplines springs from graduate school faculty and academic professionals removed from clinical or K–12 settings, and I have found that much is of limited use to practitioners in the field. Teachers, mental health providers, and parents often find that while literature describing the pathological behavior of disruptive children is available in abundance, there is a dearth of instructive material on techniques for creating, introducing, and maintaining effective interventions with these children across school, clinical, and real-life settings.

Due to its realistic orientation, Dr. George Kapalka's new text, *8 Steps to Classroom Management Success,* provides a breath of fresh air to educators and mental health professionals searching for practical strategies to deal with the disruptive child. Dr. Kapalka provides realistic vignettes illustrating problem behavior in the classroom, which will have the ring of truth to any frontline practitioner who reads them. He clearly identifies the many variables at play in disruptive classroom situations and explains how each can be manipulated to influence outcomes. With particular skill, he illuminates often-overlooked ecological variables, such as the emotional histories of teacher-student encounters; the mental preparedness that teachers bring to disciplinary situations;

and the ability of teachers and mental health practitioners to perceive and ultimately monitor their own physiological responses during disciplinary interventions.

Dr. Kapalka demonstrates the best and most efficient ways to use commands in disruptive classroom situations without escalating the tension of the moment. He not only outlines methods for issuing effective warnings, but also analyzes why most traditional warning strategies almost always fail. He discusses the use of time out strategies, clarifying how to differentiate them based on whether an outburst is violent or nonviolent. He gives examples for structuring behavioral contracts and explains how to translate teacher expectations considering the age of the child, the environment where the outburst occurred, and the baseline behaviors involved into contractual terms.

Finally, Dr. Kapalka discusses how teachers and school psychologists can transfer behavioral gains from the classroom to other school and home environments, illustrating how to implement his techniques in cafeteria and playground settings by preparing the disruptive student with clear expectations and consequences. He goes on to demonstrate how these strategies, paired with consistent parental involvement, can be used to develop effective homework methods.

As a clinical child psychologist and school psychologist who has worked for over 20 years with disruptive children in a plethora of school and clinical settings, Dr. Kapalka brings a wealth of experience to his writings. His strategies for successful interventions are based on both his experience and the most current research in the field. *8 Steps to Classroom Management Success* is a valuable tool for today's classroom teachers, school psychologists tackling the problems of the most challenged students, and parents who struggle daily to keep their children focused on appropriate behavior and tasks. I highly recommend it.

Margaret Alvarez, PsyD, MSCP, MS IV

College of Medicine and Health Sciences

Touro College, NYC

Acknowledgments

The author would like to express his gratitude to New Harbinger Publications for allowing him to reprint limited portions of his book, *Parenting Your Out-of-Control Child: An Effective, Easy-to-Use Program for Teaching Self-Control* (Kapalka, 2007d).

Additionally, Corwin would like to acknowledge the following peer reviewers for their editorial insight and guidance:

Beverly E. S. Alfeld, MA, MFA
Educational Consultant
Crystal Lake, IL

Sandra E. Archer
National Board Certified Teacher
Volusia County Schools
Ormond Beach, FL

Sally J. Coghlan, MA, NBCT
Special Education Department Chair
Rio Linda Junior High School
Rio Linda, CA

Dolores Hennessy
Reading Specialist
Sarah Noble Intermediate School
New Milford, CT

Kathy Lineberger
Media Specialist
Marvin Ward Elementary School
Winston-Salem, NC

Nancy H. McDonough
Teacher
Walter Stillman School
Tenafly, NJ

Pamela L. Opel, NBCT
Science Curriculum Specialist
Gulfport School District
Gulfport, MS

Renee Ponce-Nealon
Kindergarten Teacher, National Board Certified Teacher
McDowell Elementary School
Petaluma, CA

About the Author

 **George Kapalka** is a Board-Certified Clinical Psychologist, a Licensed Mental Health Counselor, and a Certified School Psychologist. He holds additional board certifications in child mental health services, learning disabilities, and psychopharmacology. For over 20 years, he has been an active clinician who primarily treats children and adolescents with problem behaviors. In addition, he is an associate professor of psychological counseling at Monmouth University (a Graduate Faculty appointment) and a member of the medical staff at Meridian Health Systems, where he trains physicians and nurses about the diagnosis and treatment of children with attention deficit/hyperactivity disorder (ADHD) and other disruptive disorders. Dr. Kapalka has authored books and dozens of professional publications in psychological, educational, and medical literature. In addition, he has authored or coauthored numerous research presentations at regional, national, and international conferences of psychological, educational, and medical associations. He is an active lecturer, has appeared on television, and has been quoted in news articles in stories pertaining to the development, education, and treatment of children and adolescents.

CORWIN

A SAGE Company

The Corwin logo—a raven striding across an open book—represents the union of courage and learning. Corwin is committed to improving education for all learners by publishing books and other professional development resources for those serving the field of PreK–12 education. By providing practical, hands-on materials, Corwin continues to carry out the promise of its motto: **"Helping Educators Do Their Work Better."**

Introduction

Why Do Students Misbehave?

Mrs. Smith is a second-grade teacher. She teaches a group of 25 children, including Barry, an active youngster who frequently gets into conflicts with other children. The class is just finishing spelling, and it is time for a short recess. Today, the children will stay in the classroom and play with games available to them in the back of the room. There are five computers in the classroom, so five students will have an opportunity to play games on them while the rest will break into small groups and play with board games.

As children begin to break into groups, the teacher is gathering the materials she just used to teach the preceding subject. Barry runs to the back of the classroom. He approaches a child who has selected a computer to play with and attempts to commandeer it. The other boy does not give up, and an argument between the two boys ensues, including some pushing. The teacher yells across the room,

"What's going on there?"

Barry yells, "I want to play!"

The other boy chimes in, "But I got here first!"

"Barry, he got there first, so please let him stay on," says the teacher.

Barry yells, "Nooo, I really want to play!"

The teacher approaches Barry and leads him away from the computer. He yells even louder, "Nooo, you can't make me!"

The teacher places Barry in the corner by the building blocks. In anger, he starts to throw the blocks around the room.

The teacher yells, "Stop that!" She returns to her desk to finish what she was doing.

After a moment, Barry goes over to a group of children that just started to play with a board game. He wants to join them, but they already assigned all available spots for the game and tell him he can't play. He goes over to one girl sitting on the side and gets in front of her.

The other children start to yell at him, "No, get away from here!"

Barry swipes his hand across the board, knocking all the pieces to the floor.

The teacher goes over and says, "I told you to stop! Now you have to behave! Go over there, sit down, and read a book!"

Barry protests, "Nooo! It's not fair! I want to play!"

The teacher asks the class whether any group will accept Barry. No one responds. The teacher goes over to one group of children and asks that they let Barry join them. They protest but agree.

As Barry and the group play with the game, Barry attempts to take over the game in the manner in which he likes (not in accordance with the stated rules). Every few moments, when things do not go his way, Barry acts up again. The other children try to shush him, to no avail. Throughout the 25-minute recess, the teacher must frequently go back and intervene with Barry, proclaiming, "I said knock it off!"

As the recess comes to an end, the teacher asks the children to return to their assigned seats. Barry is the last one still in the back of the room. While the children return to their desks, Barry starts to build a tower with the building blocks.

The teacher addresses Barry from across the classroom: "Barry, put those away and return to your seat."

Barry replies, "In a minute."

The teacher starts giving out a handout with a math assignment. Barry is still playing with the blocks. The teacher says, "Barry, I said put those away and come back to your desk."

"But I just want to finish building the tower!" Barry says.

The other children start working, and the teacher starts to circulate around the room to see if anyone needs help. Barry is still playing.

She raises her voice: "Barry, your work is waiting here for you." He responds, "I'm not finished!"

The teacher answers a question from another student and realizes that Barry is still in the back of the room. She tells Barry, "Come to your desk now, or I'll have to tell your mother you're not listening."

Barry does not respond. The teacher, still in the front of the room, answers another student's question and then yells, "Barry, did you hear me? I am calling your mother!"

Barry does not respond and continues to build.

The teacher, now visibly angry, marches toward Barry, starts to take the blocks out of his hands, and pulls him toward his desk. Barry starts yelling and crying: "But I was not finished! It's not fair!" He throws the blocks he still has in his hand across the room.

He gets to his desk, still crying, and his noise is disrupting the other students in the classroom.

After a minute or two, he calms down and turns around to ask the neighbor behind him a question. Other students become distracted and say, "Barry, be quiet!"

The teacher walks over to Barry, who turns toward her. The teacher directs him to do his work. He engages for the moment, but as soon as the teacher walks away, he starts to ask a neighbor to his right for a pencil. The neighbor says, "Barry, stop!" The teacher walks over to Barry.

"What do you need?" she asks.

"I don't have anything to write with," Barry says.

"Where is your pencil?" the teacher asks.

"I don't know," Barry replies.

The teacher gives Barry a pencil, directs him to work, and walks away. After a moment, Barry gets up from his desk and walks to the back of the classroom. "Where are you going?" asks the teacher. He replies, "To sharpen my pencil."

Barry gets to the pencil sharpener and sharpens his pencil loudly and repeatedly. He then starts to walk back. Passing the first desk, he starts to ask his friend a question. The two start talking. The neighbor in the front turns around and says, "Be quiet!"

The teacher walks back toward Barry and his friend. She asks, "What are you talking about?"

He replies, "I had to ask him whether he will come over later to play."

"Now?" the teacher asks.

"But I won't see him later!" Barry replies. The teacher, exasperated, directs Barry to get back to his desk. He complies and starts to work on the sheet, but two minutes later, he again starts bothering his neighbor. The teacher walks over toward Barry and says, "What are you doing?"

"I did not know how to do this one," he replies.

"Then ask me, and I'll help you." The teacher shows him and he again begins to work. A moment later, he again turns to the neighbor and starts whispering. Both boys start giggling. The girl next to them says, "Why don't you knock it off?"

The teacher walks over, but Barry sees her coming and returns to his work. Another few minutes go by.

Barry gets the attention of the teacher and says, "Psst, I want to ask you a question."

The teacher, thinking he needs help, walks over and says, "What is it?"

Barry says, "Tomorrow, can I be the first one to play on the computer?"

"We'll see," says the teacher. "Now get back to work."

He does, for a few moments, after which he again loses focus and becomes distracted. This pattern continues through the whole day.

Does this sound familiar? Perhaps the following example is closer to your experience.

Mr. Spears is a ninth-grade social studies teacher. He has 35 students in his class, including a young woman, Traci, who seems to know how to push his buttons. She dresses suggestively and enjoys the attention her male peers seem to give her. She usually arrives to class a couple of minutes late and makes a "grand entrance," obviously asking to be noticed. One day, as some of the boys in the room started catcalling, one girl yelled out, "Slut." Traci heard that and stormed toward the girl, yelling at her, "What did you say, bitch?" A friend held Traci back, and eventually she walked back to her desk and sat down.

However, this is hardly the end of the problems. Mr. Spears asks the students to take out their homework assignments. Traci does not have hers. When he asks her why, she says, "Because I didn't feel like it. Social studies is boring."

"That's a zero!" the teacher says.

"I don't care!" Traci responds.

Mr. Spears attempts to go on with his class. However, Traci starts humming to herself. The teacher says, "Traci, please stop making noise."

Traci rolls her eyes but stops. A few moments later, however, she leans over to a classmate, and both start talking and giggling. The teacher says, "Stop that laughing and pay attention!" Traci ignores him and continues to talk and laugh.

Mr. Spears yells, "I said stop!" Traci says, "All right, all right." She becomes quiet for a few minutes. However, she takes out a magazine and starts reading it. Another student tells the teacher, "Mr. Spears, Traci is reading a magazine." The teacher, thinking that he must address this or risk losing control over his classroom, goes over to Traci and says, "What are you doing?"

"Nothing," Traci responds.

"Give me the magazine" the teacher says.

"No! It's not yours, you can't take it away from me" Traci says.

"But you can't read it in class," the teacher responds.

"OK, I'll put it away," Traci says.

Traci loudly shoves the magazine inside her desk and rolls her eyes, but she does not reengage in the class discussion. After a few moments, she starts to look out the window and loudly drums on her desk with a pencil. The teacher yells to her, "Stop that!" She again rolls her eyes but becomes quiet for a moment. She then yawns, stretches her arms, and loudly proclaims, "I'm bored," after which the class bursts into laughter.

Perceiving another challenge from Traci, the teacher yells, "If you don't knock it off, I will call your parents." Traci replies, "Go ahead. They're divorced. They don't care!"

Mr. Spears does his best to continue with the class lecture and discussion, and Traci continues to occasionally disrupt. Each time he scolds her, she stops for a moment and then starts again. Mr. Spears feels very frustrated by the situation and dreads each class where Traci is present. Secretly, he wishes she would stop attending his class.

Perhaps you've experienced similar problems yourself. Perhaps you've talked with colleagues who experience these problems with their students. What went wrong in these examples? Why didn't the disruptive students listen? Could the teachers have done something to improve the likelihood that they would listen? The answers to these questions are complex and involve a combination of many factors, such as the students' basic personality, the behavioral habits they have developed, and the behaviors of the teachers.

Judging from both students' behavior, we can safely assume that both have tendencies to ignore teachers' commands and that they may also have problems transitioning from one behavior to another. Perhaps the teachers' approach in these examples would have worked with most ordinary students, but these examples involve two students who appear to be difficult and with whom the ordinary way of doing things may not work. Thus, a different approach becomes necessary.

Many teachers feel that just because they are the teacher in the classroom, students should automatically recognize that their word is law and must be obeyed. Although some students today still respond to this philosophy and listen accordingly, many do not. This approach may have worked many years ago, but times are different now. Most students today won't listen to teachers just because they say so. Most students today need a reason to listen to their teachers, one that is more substantial than "Because I said so."

Why Students Misbehave

Why are some students so difficult to manage? In the examples presented earlier, a number of factors contributed to noncompliance; some pertain to the student, some have to do with the teacher's behaviors and reactions, and some are related to classroom dynamics. It is important to consider the specifics of all of those factors to guide us toward developing an approach that will effectively address classroom behavior problems.

Student Factors

Some personality factors make it more likely that a student will exhibit difficult behaviors. Of these, impulsivity is the most notable. The more prone students are to quick reactions without much forethought, the more likely they are to misbehave. When confronted with a situation in which we don't get our way, we all experience a negative reaction. Those who are not particularly impulsive possess the ability to think through the situation, evaluate response choices and the consequences of each option, and select a behavior that results in the most desired consequences. Unfortunately, individuals who are impulsive spend little time thinking through the consequences of their behaviors and act too quickly. Often, those actions result in negative consequences that the individual didn't anticipate, and the result is a negative reaction, including frustration and anger.

Impulsivity is the result of many factors, most significantly the underactivity of the brain's frontal lobes. In its most notable form, this underactivity causes psychological disorders such as attention deficit/hyperactivity disorder. It is important to remember, however, that impulsive students don't necessarily have a psychological disorder.

Although extreme impulsivity is a sign of a more serious problem and most likely requires appropriate treatment, many students exhibit less severe symptoms of impulsivity that, nevertheless, result in behavioral difficulties. In general, impulsive individuals exhibit limited self-control; their diminished ability to think through the consequences of their behaviors often results in their inability to adapt to situations that don't turn out as they would like. Thus, impulsive students are known to have difficulties with thinking through their actions and often exhibit behaviors characterized by limited self-control.

What makes impulsivity particularly troubling is the way in which it interferes with the person's ability to learn from experience. When required to choose a behavior in a particular situation, those with sufficient ability to stop and think before they act are able to process the situation long enough to recall similar situations, the behavior they chose in the past, and the consequences they experienced. This allows them to learn from these situations. When faced with a similar choice, they can select a response that worked best in the past (or, at least, stop selecting the behavior that generally resulted in negative consequences).

However, impulsive students with limited self-control don't think through each situation sufficiently to recall prior experiences, so they are much more likely to repeat the same poor choices. This point is very important to remember: Impulsive students require repeated exposure to consistent consequences before they eventually begin to think before they act and start to learn from previous experience.

The Strong-Willed Student

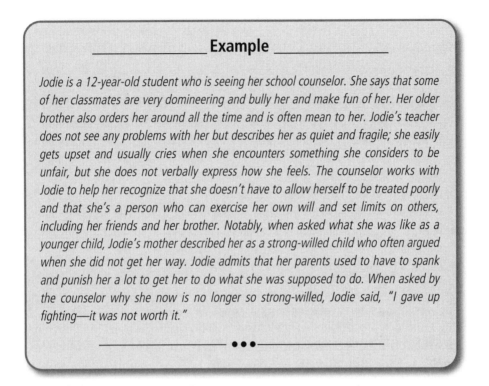

Example

Jodie is a 12-year-old student who is seeing her school counselor. She says that some of her classmates are very domineering and bully her and make fun of her. Her older brother also orders her around all the time and is often mean to her. Jodie's teacher does not see any problems with her but describes her as quiet and fragile; she easily gets upset and usually cries when she encounters something she considers to be unfair, but she does not verbally express how she feels. The counselor works with Jodie to help her recognize that she doesn't have to allow herself to be treated poorly and that she's a person who can exercise her own will and set limits on others, including her friends and her brother. Notably, when asked what she was like as a younger child, Jodie's mother described her as a strong-willed child who often argued when she did not get her way. Jodie admits that her parents used to have to spank and punish her a lot to get her to do what she was supposed to do. When asked by the counselor why she now is no longer so strong-willed, Jodie said, "I gave up fighting—it was not worth it."

Example

Mike is a 16-year-old student who is currently on home-bound instruction. Mike is unable to attend regular classroom instruction. He has attended different classroom settings, including inclusion and self-contained placements, but none have worked. Mike admits that he does not get along with teachers: "When they start ordering me around, I tell them off and then I walk out." Mike and his parents frequently get into arguments because he challenges them when he doesn't get his own way. He has two siblings and he fights with them all the time, sometimes including physical altercations. Mike has few friends and similarly argues with them whenever they do not do what he wants. In counseling, Mike voluntarily admits that he does not get along with most people: "Everyone has been trying to run my life ever since I was a child. I can't stand it."

Example

Charlie is an 18-year-old high school senior. Two years ago, Charlie had an idea that high school students need a way to send instant messages as a group rather than individually. Similar to a chat room, he felt that groups of teenagers should be able to have a simple platform on which to establish electronic interactions, just as easy as it is to start talking when a group of friends gets together. He approached major Internet companies, but they did not like his ideas and felt that the services already offered by giants like Google and Yahoo! were similar enough that there was too small a market for what he sought. However, Charlie did not give up. He obtained a loan from a local bank and set up his own computer servers in the garage. He then marketed the idea to students in his high school and obtained enough interest that his efforts attracted one sponsor, who now advertises on his service. Along the way, Charlie's efforts also resulted in interest from colleges, and he just secured a grant that will pay for almost all of his expenses at a well-known college next year. Charlie's parents remark that they respect his strength and determination: "He's always been that way. When he sets his mind to do something, no one can stop him. He still gets upset when things don't go his way." However, they also say that he seems to know when to let go. His mother says, "Somehow, he's learned not to sweat the small stuff."

● ● ●

What do these three students have in common? One obvious similarity is that they all had tendencies to be strong-willed. These tendencies, however, progressed differently as they became teenagers. For Jodie, her defiance and strong will were squelched. Mike's defiance was exacerbated and eventually started to rule his life. For Charlie, the strong-willed nature became an asset, and he was able to use it constructively.

If these three students started out with similar personalities, what accounts for their different paths? The answer lies, at least partially, in the manner in which their strong-willed natures evolved during development. Jodie's spirit was broken, and she learned that it wasn't worth it to stand up for herself and attempt to have things in life go her way. Mike's defiant tendencies intensified, and he now always seeks to get his own way, although it is obviously to his detriment in school, at home, and with friends. Charlie, on the other hand, seemed able to retain strength of will and perseverance to get his own way when it really matters while having the good judgment to "stop sweating the small stuff."

How do we, as teachers, affect the way in which our students grow as people? We must start by recognizing that some strength of will is an asset to a person. For it to remain a strength rather than a liability, however, students must develop the ability to judge a situation and determine when persisting to get their own way is likely to be beneficial, and when it is counterproductive and will probably result in negative consequences. As teachers, we don't want our students to lose their resolve and become like Jodie. Likewise, we hope that our students won't be like Mike. Instead, we want our students to retain strength of will and perseverance while moderating it with good judgment, like Charlie. Before I cover the approach that will guide teachers to help students develop better judgment, it is important to consider teacher factors that contribute to problem situations.

Teacher Factors

The overwhelming majority of teachers are education professionals who want to help their students become smart and successful. When students' behaviors interfere with teaching, this makes teachers frustrated because they feel that it prevents them from accomplishing these goals. When frustrated, many teachers lose control over their own reactions and a conflict ensues. Consequently, helping teachers manage their own reactions is an important component of effective student behavior management. To do so, we must start with clarifying the most basic component that underlies teachers' beliefs and expectations, the goals that the teachers set for themselves as education professionals.

The Goals of Teaching

During speaking engagements, I'm often asked about the goals of teaching and the best ways to achieve them. This is obviously a complex question with many answers, but generally I think that teachers mainly have the obligation to facilitate their students' growth and development and to prepare them for adulthood. Although academic achievement and skill building in the major academic areas are part of these larger goals, the focus on growth and development and on preparation for adulthood is more important than any grade or test score.

The first of these goals, facilitating growth and development, is attained through providing an environment in which the students' educational and emotional needs are met. The educational needs are met by creating a setting conducive to learning, exposing students to academic tasks that foster the development of cognitive skills, offering challenge and stimulation to facilitate growth, and encouraging and monitoring students' progress. The emotional needs, however, are more elusive, although no less important. These include the ability to communicate caring, empathy, and respect for students as individuals and worthwhile human beings. Here, teachers must recognize that students develop their own personalities, even if those personalities are different from those with which the teachers are comfortable.

The other goal, that of preparing students for adulthood, has many facets. Essentially, what we want to accomplish as teachers is to help students develop a set of life skills that will help them function as well-adjusted adults. Many specific skills contribute to this desirable outcome, but the development of good self-control is perhaps most crucial.

Teacher Expectations

_____ **Example** _____

David is a sixth-grade teacher who is seeking advice from the vice principal about one of his students, John. The student doesn't listen to what David tells him and says things like, "No, I don't have to," and "You can't make me." The teacher admits that this makes him very angry. He can't stand the defiance and views it as a direct assault on his authority as a teacher. It isn't the student's place to question anything that the teacher says. In other words, "Students must obey because I say so. When we were in school, we would have never defied our teachers because our parents would beat the crap out of us. If John was my son, I would never go for this. I think John is this way because his parents don't care and they failed to teach him respect."

_____ ●●● _____

All too common, this example exhibits some disturbing trends. First, the teacher expects blind obedience from his students and views the student's misbehavior as a deliberate attempt to usurp the teacher's authority. In addition, it places primary blame outside of the current situation, on the student's parents. Not only is this approach counterproductive to the process of developing constructive solutions, but it also erodes the teacher's relationship with the student's parents, as the underlying assumptions about the parents' failings set negative expectations. In other words, this approach assumes that, "The parents are at fault, and if they don't do anything, there is nothing I can do about it."

In the previous section, when asked about Jodie, Mike, or Charlie, most teachers would likely choose Charlie as a model of how they would like their students to evolve. However, the teachers' perceptions of how such an outcome comes about is often inaccurate. On one hand, they want their students to accept blindly everything that they tell them to do; on the other hand, they expect the students to develop simultaneously the ability to stand up for what they believe and be able to exert strong will as adults. These two expectations are contradictory. A student who blindly accepts everything that teachers say will *not* become an adult who is independently minded and tenacious. The ability to persevere and try to get one's own way starts early in life and will not evolve if squelched. No student can magically become a strong and persistent adult without developing these tendencies gradually in childhood and adolescence.

The Role of Judgment

We all want our students to develop into smart, well-adjusted, and strong adults. We want them to learn to think for themselves and make the right decisions, but we must recognize that the journey to attaining these goals starts very early. The way we manage behaviors has a lot to do with the degree to which children and adolescents become happy, well adjusted, and strong adults. If a student is scorned every time he expresses his own will, the eventual result will be an adult who is unhappy, feels poorly about himself, and lacks self-confidence. In other words, the students will become like Jodie. This doesn't mean that the misbehaviors should go unchecked. If your students don't learn to use good judgment, they may grow up to be like Mike. How, then, do we balance our approach and help our students develop to become adults like Charlie?

One way to do so is to focus on the behavior rather than the attitude. In other words, don't expect your student to do what you say blindly, without any objection. Even though your job as a teacher may be easier, you're much more likely to turn your student into a passive adult. Instead, expect your student to question what you ask or command, and don't view this as a test of your authority.

Remember, your student is still learning how to differentiate settings in which exerting her own will is desirable from those in which it is not. If you want your student to become a self-confident and mentally strong adult, the journey in that direction starts in youth, in our classrooms. Don't squelch the strong will. Don't punish your student for the initial reluctance or refusal.

What your student does is much more important than what he says. (There are exceptions addressed later in this book.) If the student exhibited reluctance or protest but still made the right choice of behavior, don't punish or scold him for the initial reaction. If he made the wrong choice of behavior, allow the consequences to become the tool by which he eventually learns to make a better choice. Unless his words were abusive, what he said along the way is mostly irrelevant.

Keep in mind that you do not want to break your student's spirit. You want to encourage her attempts to exercise her will, but you also want her to learn the difference between doing so all the time and doing so when it is necessary and proper. In other words, you want your student to have a choice about whether to comply with your command or request. In this manner, your student will learn self-control. You want your student to comply with your command because she knows the consequences of complying and not complying and because she decided which of these consequences she desires. Your goal is not to force compliance but to teach your student the consequences of complying versus not complying. This is a crucial distinction.

If your student doesn't listen, this does not mean that you weren't successful as a teacher. Your job is to teach (and administer) proper consequences, and you can do this regardless of whether your student complied with your command. If your student does not comply, you haven't failed. You would have failed only if you didn't administer appropriate consequences.

If you can clearly establish the parameters beforehand, especially with regard to the consequences that your student will experience after either an appropriate or inappropriate behavior, you will eventually teach your student to make the right choices, and this book will help you do so. This teaches your student to exercise reasoning and judgment. This point is so important that keeping just this point in mind, even if you don't follow anything else in this book, will make a significant difference in how you interact with your students and what you expect of them. This will help them grow up to be happier and better adjusted individuals.

How Can This Book Help Me?

You have just learned some of the reasons why students exhibit behavioral problems. However, just understanding those reasons is not enough to change things. In this book, you will also learn how to control your own emotional reactions so that you remain calmer. The more you control yourself and your own reactions, the more effective you will become in successfully managing your students' behaviors. Breaking the cycle of escalation will allow you to remain in control and therefore short-circuit the spiral that leads to most confrontations.

This book will help you give your students reasons why they should listen to you and help them understand what will happen when they do or don't listen. You will learn how to identify and implement proper consequences for your students' positive and negative behaviors. Throughout the book, there are examples of common behavioral problems that teachers experience. With each, I'll help you understand what went wrong and why the student acted out. You will develop necessary strategies to reduce acting out and increase the degree of control you have over your students' behaviors.

What Can I Expect From This Book?

Please understand that there are no quick fixes, and no strategy in the world will instantly turn a difficult student into a compliant one. Improving the situation is possible, but it will require work, effort, and a commitment of your time. This book offers you a set of tools that have been shown to be effective in reducing behavioral problems, but these tools need time to work, and you'll need to use them consistently.

To further expand on that point, please don't approach the strategies described in this book with a wait-and-see attitude. That is, please don't say "I'll try to use these to see if they will work." This kind of approach will almost surely destine you to failure. The methods in this book will only work if you have enough faith in them to alter the way in which you address your students on a permanent basis.

Start with a conclusion that you are ready to do something different, something that will help you turn things around with your students. If you are like the typical teacher, you probably have already tried everything you could think of, and nothing has worked. So, what do you have to lose? Have faith. The procedures in this book will make a difference, although the amount of change you can expect varies from student to student. If you are willing to commit the effort and perseverance required to implement the following strategies, you'll see results.

You'll also need to give it a commitment of time. Learning new habits, skills, and techniques is a laborious process. Although this book is divided into manageable steps, each of which most teachers can easily accomplish in a typical week or two, obtaining long-term change takes time and perseverance. Do not try to proceed too quickly. Give each step enough time to work and begin to produce at least some positive results.

How Do I Know This Program Is Effective?

The program contained in this book was developed in the 1990s. As a clinical child psychologist and a school psychologist for nearly two decades, I have worked often with difficult youngsters, in and out of school settings. Teachers of those students need help to break the escalation patterns that are so common with many of those students. For many years, resources have existed for clinicians to help parents and teachers implement strategies that reduce conflicts and improve the manageability of difficult children and adolescents. For example, behavioral contracting has long been known to be effective. Available resources for parents and teachers, however, rarely provide the kind of detailed instructions that assist them in developing an effective behavior contract, and a poorly implemented contract is not likely to be very effective. Thus, I began to identify those components of behavioral contracting that appear to make it most likely to be successful.

Clinicians working with defiant children often follow a program designed by Russell Barkley (1997). I found components of this program helpful, but also in my experience, revising the program made it more effective within school settings. Gradually, I significantly expanded the program, revised certain steps, and added others. Consequently, components of the program contained in this book are loosely based on Barkley's work, with significant additions and changes that are specifically relevant to teachers.

Once this new program was complete, I performed several studies to research its effectiveness. Each step of the technique was researched, and the results are available in professional literature (Kapalka 2005a, 2005b, 2007a, 2008a; Kapalka & Bryk, 2007) or were presented at professional conferences (Kapalka, 2001, 2005c, 2005d, 2006, 2007b, 2007c, 2008b) and are being prepared for publication. The studies revealed that each step resulted in a 25% to 65% reduction in behavioral problems. When you consider the combined effect of utilizing many of the steps, the overall reduction in problems was very significant. Thus, you can be confident that the program you are reading is based on sound psychological principles and is backed by empirical, scientific evidence of its effectiveness. In addition, you can expect that the more steps you implement, the greater the benefit that you will experience.

How Do I Use This Book?

This book describes a behavior management program that involves the use of eight separate but related techniques that collectively will help you bring your students under control. Each step is designed to address a specific problem that students commonly exhibit when acting out. The steps must be mastered individually, and you must be comfortable with using a step on a daily basis before you proceed to the next one. Although the steps each address a different problem, they build upon one another; you need to truly master Step 1 before you proceed to Step 2, you must have mastered Steps 1 and 2 before you should proceed to Step 3, and so on. Consequently, it is recommended that you only attempt one step every one to two weeks. In this way, you'll give yourself and your students enough time to get used to the new way of doing things, and you'll then be ready to proceed to the next step.

The steps are designed to work in sequence. The sequence of steps is not accidental; it is designed to help you master the steps in order because each step builds upon the steps you master before it. Consequently, please don't jump around and try to pick and choose the specific interventions you want to use with your students. You may get some benefit from doing so, but the program won't be nearly as effective. Instead, master all of the steps, in sequence. Once you have completed Steps 1 through 4, you may then pick and choose whether any or all of the remaining steps will be useful, and you can administer those in any order, as needed.

Each of the steps is accompanied by summary checklists. These sheets are intended to be used as reminders to keep you on track. As you proceed through each step, place the sheets in a conspicuous place where they will act as reminders to you. Spontaneously coming across them as you go through your day of teaching will help you remember the details of each technique. The more you consult them, the more success you will experience with the implementation of each step.

Finally, please don't skip the first chapter and proceed directly to the behavioral program. Although you can derive some benefit from the program even if you don't read the next chapter, your administration of the steps won't be as effective. As a teacher, your success in bringing your students under control depends on several factors. Not only must you gain some understanding of why your students are behaving the way they do, but you must also understand why you react the way you do and what specifically you need to change about your own reactions to become more effective as a disciplinarian. So, roll up your sleeves and get ready to start on this important journey.

Prologue

Prepare Yourself

Two teachers leave a meeting of the Board of Education. They both hoped to persuade the Board to fund their programs. One got the funding, the other did not. One teacher says to the other, "I'm sorry I lost my temper. I guess I care about my program so much that my emotions got the best of me. Congratulations on getting your funding. I'm a little surprised, though. I thought that, ultimately, the program I supported was more beneficial to our district." The other teacher replies, "Perhaps you're right; I don't know. However, the side that stays calm is usually the side that is in control."

This vignette, an adaptation of an anecdote I heard once from an attorney (see Kapalka, 2007d, Chapter 2), illustrates a principle that is well known to those who work in professions and occupations that involve negotiations and conflict resolution (e.g., legal, law enforcement, legislative). Although frustration is a normal human reaction, those who experience intense anger have difficulty thinking clearly. Conversely, those who stay calm and remain in charge of their faculties usually end up being more effective in arguing their point. In other words, as you attend to your students' misbehaviors, you need to stay calm—but how do you do that when your students continually challenge your authority? To remain in control of your reactions, you'll need to understand how the anger response develops in your mind and body. This will help you develop the skills you need to manage your anger and prevent it from overtaking your senses.

The Emotional Reaction

Our brain is prewired to react similarly to strong emotions (e.g., anxiety and anger). When we face an oppositional student, the brain goes through reactions similar to those when we face physical danger. Let's review the steps involved in our experience of emotions.

Stimulus

The stimulus is not something over which we usually have control. It happens, like a charging lion or a frustrating student, and we must deal with it when it does. This is the first stage of our emotional response, and the remaining stages quickly follow.

Interpretation

Once we become aware of the stimulus, we immediately process the situation to interpret its meaning and importance. If that interpretation leads to a conclusion that we are being threatened, we act accordingly.

Physiological Arousal

Once a stimulus is identified as one that requires action, our body must mobilize its physical resources to be able to act in the most effective way. The sympathetic nervous system awakens and activates parts of the body that increase physical arousal to maximize our ability to perform an action. This physiological arousal includes the increase in blood pressure and heartbeat, redistribution of blood flow away from digestive organs and into muscles, sweating (to accommodate the increased metabolism in the muscles), pupil dilation, and an increase in respiration to oxygenate the blood. In summary, we physically get ready to face the challenge.

Response

With the body prepared for action, we next select a behavior. Usually, this becomes an all-or-nothing response as the body completes the chosen action as quickly and efficiently as possible. Thus, what happens after we become aware of the stimulus (interpretation, physiological arousal, and selecting a response) is collectively known as the *fight–flight* reaction.

Preparation

Actually, two more components need to be included in the process. Preparation is really the initial phase of the emotional reaction. If we expect to be challenged or threatened, we usually maintain a calm state of overall arousal, and switching into the fight–flight mode may take a little longer. Conversely, when we expect danger or frustration, we are already on edge, and we are more likely to interpret events as requiring the fight–flight reaction.

Consequence

Our experience with outcomes of similar situations we've experienced in the past affects our behavior in the future. If we encountered a challenge but were able to conquer it, we will approach similar settings with a sense of confidence and comfort in knowing that we can handle them successfully. However, if a situation repeatedly challenges us and our ability to respond seems limited, we learn to expect the worst and experience much more baseline arousal when we encounter it again. This higher arousal makes it more likely that we will experience a fight–flight reaction in that setting.

Thus, when we talk about an emotional reaction, we must really consider six stages: preparation, stimulus, interpretation, physiological arousal, response, and consequence.

The Emotional Reaction of a Frustrated Teacher

In this book, the specific response of most interest to us is the anger and frustration that a teacher feels when faced with students who protest and refuses to do what they are told. Let's revisit the example of Barry and his teacher (Mrs. Smith), discussed in the Introduction, and identify the stages of emotional reaction that Mrs. Smith likely experienced.

Preparation

To start, the teacher was already expecting to have difficulties with Barry, and she likely was dreading the interaction. She probably recalled previous problems she encountered with him in similar situations and remembered the conflict and confrontation that often ensued. Probably, she already started the interaction with him by thinking, "This will be trouble, here we go again, why do I always have to go through this with him?" Thus, in the first stage of her emotional reaction, she had already prepared herself for yet another bad incident with Barry.

In addition, her prior feelings of frustration exacerbated her negative mindset. She likely felt upset that she had been failing to control her student, which made her feel angry. Teachers who have a difficult, oppositional student in their classroom often attribute the problems, at least in part, to their own failure to bring the student under control.

This belief further escalates the frustration and anger toward the student, and every additional problem serves as yet another reminder of the teacher's failure to control the student. Such mental "preparation" made it even more likely that she would react negatively to Barry's behavior, even if he really didn't act out in a major way.

Most likely, Mrs. Smith's body language and voice intonation signaled to Barry that she was already on edge. In turn, Barry probably reacted in kind, and this accelerated his escalation. Oppositional students are particularly sensitive to tense feelings and respond negatively when they encounter them (as observed, e.g., by Barkley, Fischer, Edelbrock, & Smallish, 1991). The more edgy and annoyed you appear when approaching your students, the more likely they are to respond aggressively, as if to "fight fire with fire." Consequently, confrontations will probably occur.

Stimulus

In the example in the Introduction, next came the stimulus—Barry's defiance, but careful examination of the sequence of events reveals that Barry was not defiant at first. Yes, he was reluctant to obey, but he didn't openly defy. The defiance became more evident as he escalated. Thus, the stimulus was really noncompliance, not defiance, although the teacher may not have interpreted it as such.

Interpretation

In the teacher's mind, Barry was at it again, and Mrs. Smith likely expected to have a problem with him, so she interpreted his response as a confirmation of her expectations. This interpretation escalated the situation further. Because she expected the worst, anything that Barry did confirmed those expectations. Short of saying "yes," almost any behavior that Barry exhibited was going to be interpreted by her as a sign of trouble. That interpretation, however, may not have been entirely accurate, and it unnecessarily escalated the situation.

Physiological Arousal

As Mrs. Smith became more angry, her physiological arousal amplified—her blood pressure and heart rate increased, her breathing became more rapid and shallow, and she experienced a boost of adrenaline (that may not have been consciously perceptible) that made her more ready for action. When a person is within such a state of arousal, she's physiologically and mentally ready to strike. As that state progresses, it becomes more difficult to respond rationally. The person becomes more ready for a battle, and even minor annoyances precipitate an explosion.

Response

As the teacher responded to Barry's behavior with increased frustration, he picked up on her anger and also escalated his behavior. As the teacher got angrier, he reacted in kind. Eventually, the two of them reached a point of no return, and the situation became a confrontation. Along the way, Barry lost control over his emotions.

Consequence

We can speculate about what happened after this confrontation. Barry got yelled at yet again by his teacher, so he probably felt poorly about himself and the situation. Once again, he made her angry and unhappy, and other students expressed their disapproval as well. Although he may not understand the specifics, he likely recognized that once again he became involved in an unpleasant interaction that did not end as he would have liked it. In the future, situations like these teach him to expect the worst.

Likewise, Mrs. Smith probably experienced a negative reaction. The conflict she had expected happened again, and her feelings of frustration and anger at Barry escalated even further, so that she'll be even more ready for another battle in the future. The entire incident just proved to her that Barry is uncontrollable and will not respond positively to anything that she says or does. Once again, this only amplifies the negative expectation she will feel in the future and this mindset will increasingly permeate all of her interactions with Barry.

The Emotional Reaction of a Teacher Who Remains in Control

How do teachers break this cycle? There are effective methods of intervening in each of the six stages of emotional response to make a difference in how teachers react. Even if you're able to utilize only some of these suggestions, they will help you to stay calm. When you're calm, you can think more clearly. If you're able to utilize several of the suggestions, you'll experience an even greater difference in how you react, and you'll become much more effective in managing your students' behaviors.

Preparation

To start, you must avoid preparing for a battle. As Barry's example illustrates, if you expect a battle, you'll get one. You'll interpret each thing that happens as more proof of what you expected. Instead, prepare yourself for the possibility that the situation *may* escalate. If it does, you'll have the tools necessary to stay in control. Remember the examples of the two teachers from the beginning of this chapter.

To stay calm and in control, take a few deep breaths before you approach your oppositional student. It's best to take slow, deep breaths that last about four seconds, during which you fill your lungs completely with air. Then, hold all the air in your lungs for about one second, and slowly exhale to get all the air out. When exhaling, pretend that you are holding a lit candle in front of your mouth, and exhale slowly enough so that you do not blow it out. Repeat this procedure two or three times in one minute, breathing normally in between. While doing so, say to yourself, "I will stay calm. I will not lose control no matter what he does. It will be OK. One of us has to act like a grown-up, and it will be me." Not only will doing so help you prepare yourself mentally, but you will also maintain your pulmonary and circulatory function at a slower pace, making it easier to stay calm.

It will help you to remember that your job is not to get compliance at any price but to teach your students the consequences of their actions. Even if they don't comply, you haven't lost. True, it may be less convenient if you have to pick up the toys because your students refuse, but it doesn't mean that it will always be that way or that you have failed as a teacher.

If you recognize that certain commands and situations require more time and effort on your part, don't wait until the last minute to get into the situation. If your student does not transition away from play activities easily, do not wait until the last minute to begin to do so. If you feel rushed, your student will perceive this from you and be more likely to create problems—not because he recognizes that you are vulnerable at the moment and so he can take advantage but because he will perceive an added edge in your approach that will more easily escalate his mental state. Thus, make sure to prepare yourself adequately and give yourself enough time to address situations you previously found to be difficult.

Remember that you did not cause your student's tendencies to be willful or defiant. The student's dispositional tendencies, which are usually genetic, determine many of his reactions. Your job as a teacher is to help your student develop the good judgment to moderate these characteristics and to be able to decide how much willfulness or defiance is OK to exhibit in any given situation.

Stimulus

From your vantage point, this is the one stage that you cannot control, because you can't stop your students from performing the *stimulus*—the action of saying something or doing something that is noncompliant, defiant, or otherwise inappropriate. However, even here, you can make a difference, although indirectly. By following the steps outlined in this book and remaining calm and consistent, over time you can help to diminish your students' behavioral difficulties because you will help them to develop better self-control. This, in turn, will help them process each situation and become better able to decide where to exercise their strong will.

Interpretation

This stage is absolutely crucial to successful anger control. How you interpret your students' behavior the moment that it happens will greatly determine your reaction. The more personally you take the behavior, the more likely you'll be to get angry. The more you feel that your students are misbehaving to spite you or just to get to you, the more enraged you'll become. Instead, view your students as goal-directed people who are merely trying to get their own way in the best way they know and that they easily lose control and become unable to suppress the urge to oppose.

Don't expect them to like what you tell them to do. Instead, help your students make the choice between positive and negative behaviors by helping them recognize the consequences that each choice will bring. Whatever your students' choices, as long as you administer the appropriate consequences, you have done your job as a teacher. Even if you have to pick up their items because they refused to do so, isn't a slight inconvenience worth it to be able to teach your students a valuable lesson about behaviors and consequences? Won't it give you a good feeling to know that what you are doing is preparing your students to be able to make better decisions as they get older?

Physiological Arousal

If you are successful in avoiding negative interpretations of your student's actions, you probably won't need to do much to control your physiological reaction. The body's arousal depends almost entirely on whether you interpret that there's a need for you to get angry or excited in the first place. If you don't personalize or exaggerate your student's misbehavior, you won't experience the physiological arousal that leads to an anger outburst, and you'll stay in control.

Still, if the situation becomes volatile and your student is really pushing your buttons, there are things that you can do. When physiological arousal takes place, you experience a rush that happens very quickly. Although you may not notice it when it first happens, you can recognize it if you really try. With practice, you can become aware of your breathing becoming more shallow, your voice and speech changing character (when angry, people tend to speak louder and, usually, faster), even the rush you feel as your pulse and blood pressure increase. All of these can become signals that you are angry and must do something to calm down.

When you feel these changes in your body, it's time to walk away from your student. You do not have to leave the classroom, but walk away and take a few deep breaths in the manner discussed earlier in this chapter (a cycle of inhaling for four seconds, holding for one second, and exhaling for four seconds). While doing this, suppress any negative thoughts about your student—they will only escalate your anger. Although there are times when your immediate action is necessary (e.g., when your student is about to do something dangerous), in the most common situations with your student you'll be able to delay your response for a few moments until you feel more calm. You'll make a better choice of your actions and thus be more effective. As the saying goes, "somebody has to be the grown-up."

Response

When you respond, try to be calm but deliberate. Step 1 will give you suggestions of how to address your student. Do so directly and focus on what you want your student to do. Don't personalize or comment on your student's personality. Don't bring up past conflicts. Redirect your student to think about the choice she has between positive and negative behaviors and the consequences that follow each choice. Remember, this is a teachable moment, an opportunity for your student to learn from this experience.

If your student begins to have a tantrum, do not respond with anger. Stay in control of what you say and do. Remember that she is not singling you out to give you a hard time—she is simply losing control and can no longer contain her emotions. Step 3 will help you address these situations.

Consequence

If a confrontation has occurred, stay calm and try to think about what happened. Don't allow yourself to experience thoughts such as, "Well, there he went again, I knew this would happen." Similarly, don't blame yourself or feel that you caused the confrontation. Instead, try to analyze the sequence of events. What did your student say, and how did you react? Did he catch you off guard? If so, why? Was it a behavior that never happened before, or was it that you just didn't prepare yourself adequately for something that happens regularly? If so, make a plan for how to handle this same situation when it happens again—prepare yourself, stay calm, and think about your options before you initiate the interaction. Much of what you will learn in this book will help you address these kinds of situations.

Even though whatever you did this time appeared to be ineffective, you can learn from it and try to avoid doing the same thing in the future. Accept that people (both you and your student) learn by making mistakes. Without mistakes, we don't have the opportunity to try out what works and what doesn't. If what you tried didn't work, treat it as a lesson and think of what else you can do next time.

Avoid asking, "Why is my student doing this?" Instead, ask, "What can I do about it?" This program will help you structure the student's daily routine and make the environment more predictable for him, and if you continue to administer immediate consequences for both positive and negative behaviors, in time you'll reduce behavioral problems and help your student grow up to be a better adjusted, happier adult.

The Program

The forthcoming chapters present a set of tools that will help you address the most common behavioral problems that oppositional students exhibit in the classroom. Keep in mind that you'll need to implement each step gradually, and you may not see much difference after you've implemented just one or two steps. This doesn't mean that they aren't working. Gradually, positive changes will take place that may not become apparent until after you have implemented several of the steps.

Step 1

Give Effective Single-Action Commands

After reading the preceding discussion, you should now have a greater understanding of why some students exhibit behavioral problems that are difficult to manage and what it will take to address these problems. Beginning with this chapter, you will learn techniques to tackle common trouble spots that teachers often encounter with oppositional students. As mentioned earlier, you will gain the most benefit from the following steps if you read only one chapter at a time and try to implement only one step every one to two weeks. It's best to proceed slowly. The steps are easy to implement, but you'll need time to get used to each step and to include it in your daily class routine. Each step becomes most effective when you are so familiar with it that using it becomes automatic. Likewise, your students will also need time to get used to your new management style. As I pointed out previously, students respond best when their environment is routine and predictable. Consequently, they need time to adjust and to learn what to expect from you, the teacher.

We need a starting point to begin our journey, and the most logical place is to consider the one aspect of teacher-student interaction that probably accounts for the majority of all teacher-student communication. When teachers talk to the whole class, they usually explain, demonstrate, and clarify. However, when a teacher addresses a student directly, it is most commonly to give an instruction, ask a question, or give a command. So, for the first step, let's focus mainly on two aspects of your interaction with the students:

1. How to give a command to your oppositional and defiant student

2. What to do when your student obeys the command

For starters, select some commands with which you usually have problems obtaining compliance. These should be direct, simple commands that require a single action, such as "Return to your seat," "Put away the toys; play time is over," or "Open your math book." Don't use complex commands that call for more multiple actions. The way to obtain compliance in these types of situations is addressed in later steps. For now, focus on very direct, simple commands that require a single, specific action by your students.

Let's return to the example of Barry and his teacher from the Introduction. Many problems were evident in the interaction between them, and these will have to be addressed separately. Perhaps the one problem that appeared to permeate this vignette was his noncompliance with numerous commands given by his teacher. Let's take another look at a portion of this example.

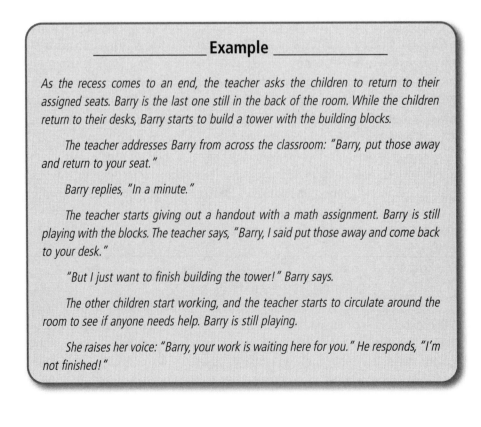

Example

As the recess comes to an end, the teacher asks the children to return to their assigned seats. Barry is the last one still in the back of the room. While the children return to their desks, Barry starts to build a tower with the building blocks.

The teacher addresses Barry from across the classroom: "Barry, put those away and return to your seat."

Barry replies, "In a minute."

The teacher starts giving out a handout with a math assignment. Barry is still playing with the blocks. The teacher says, "Barry, I said put those away and come back to your desk."

"But I just want to finish building the tower!" Barry says.

The other children start working, and the teacher starts to circulate around the room to see if anyone needs help. Barry is still playing.

She raises her voice: "Barry, your work is waiting here for you." He responds, "I'm not finished!"

The teacher answers a question from another student and realizes that Barry is still in the back of the room. She tells Barry, "Come to your desk now, or I'll have to tell your mother you're not listening."

Barry does not respond. The teacher, still in the front of the room, answers another student's question and then yells, "Barry, did you hear me? I am calling your mother!"

Barry does not respond and continues to build.

The teacher, now visibly angry, marches toward Barry, starts to take the blocks out of his hands, and pulls him toward his desk. Barry starts yelling and crying: "But I was not finished! It's not fair!" He throws the blocks he still has in his hand across the room.

He gets to his desk, still crying, and his noise is disrupting the other students in the classroom.

● ● ●

Let's analyze some aspects of this example. The teacher's attempts to direct Barry were given in the midst of other activities in the classroom. Although this probably wouldn't pose a problem for many students, Barry requires a different approach. When dealing with an impulsive, oppositional, and defiant student, the teacher should stop what she's doing, approach the student directly, and not resume any other activities until the interaction with this student has ended. While this will require more time for each specific instance, it will be time well spent, as it will improve student compliance and decrease the likelihood of conflicts.

In addition, it is apparent that Barry did not want to follow through on the stated command right from the start, and the teacher did not take any steps to help him process the situation and reconsider that choice. The teacher merely repeated the command, and the situation gradually escalated. At one point, the teacher did threaten Barry, but for reasons that are described in the next chapter, this threat was similarly ineffective. In the end, the interaction merely escalated the conflict. There must be a better way.

Well, there is, and in this chapter I describe a more effective approach. However, we must appreciate that the situation illustrated in the earlier example, although apparently simple at first glance, is rather complex and composed of discrete elements that must be examined separately. Thus, I review command giving in two chapters. In Step 1, I describe how to give a command in a manner that maximizes the likelihood of effectiveness, as confirmed by research studies with two different groups of teachers (Kapalka, 2001, 2005b). Step 2, in the next chapter, covers what to do if Step 1, when used alone, is ineffective. However, please do not try to combine Steps 1 and 2. It is really important that you give yourself sufficient time to practice Step 1 and the techniques described in this chapter before proceeding to Step 2. In addition, the procedure described herein helps you develop a new way of communicating with your student and serves as the foundation upon which further components of this program are built. Please do not simply glance over it and move on.

The Effective Command

As outlined in Step 1 Checklist at the end of this chapter, there are three components to an effective command:

1. Attentional cue

2. Command

3. Follow-up look

Let's look at each of these in detail.

The Attentional Cue

As mentioned before, you have to devote your undivided attention to your student while you attend to the command. However, you must also *get* attention from your student. In the example of Barry and his teacher, the teacher was issuing commands to him while attending to other things and did not assure that Barry attended to or processed the commands. Instead, the first thing to do before issuing a command is to get undivided attention. This is accomplished through the attentional cue.

The simplest way to cue your student to pay attention is to call his name. However, as illustrated earlier, it's not sufficient to call to the student from across the classroom. Instead, you must try to get eye contact. Walk closer to your student and call his name. If calling his name is not enough, tell him, "Look at me." If this is not sufficient, go to him and get his eye contact by adjusting your own position so that you can catch his eye or any other reasonable way that results in direct eye contact with him. As was clearly evident in the aforementioned example, long-distance commands with no eye contact almost guarantee noncompliance.

Face-to-face commands are more likely to be respected and followed. Why? There are several reasons. Human eye contact defines the interaction as one that involves mutuality, akin to a contract between two people, where the implicit understanding is that it will involve a call and response—a give and take. The listener understands the defined role of both communicators. He may not necessarily like what is being said, but he is more likely to respond to it, rather than ignore it. Although it isn't a guarantee of success, it greatly increases the likelihood of compliance, and teachers of difficult students need to stack the deck in their favor. This alone may not result in compliance, but when combined with the other techniques you'll utilize, it will certainly help.

Getting eye contact has additional benefits. Some students get so involved in an activity that they tune out much of what is going on around them. Even if they briefly acknowledge that someone is talking to them and telling them something, they are likely to pay limited attention to the content of the communication and process it very little. Students with attentional difficulties, such as attention deficit/hyperactivity disorder (ADHD), are very likely to behave in this manner. When they don't comply, it may not be an overt sign of defiance; it may be that the command you issued didn't fully register. Getting eye contact momentarily breaks what they are doing long enough for them to process what was said. Afterward, they are more likely to perform the desired behavior.

What happens when you don't get eye contact was well illustrated in the example with Barry. Most of the commands were given from across the room as the teacher attended to several other tasks. Obtaining compliance from Barry seemed no more important to the teacher than attending to those other tasks. Barry likely perceived that he really did not have to listen because the teacher was busy doing other things. It is important to point out that his response was more instinctive rather than premeditated; nevertheless, he knew that he was more likely to get away with continuing what he was doing because the teacher was occupied with other issues. Through eye contact you break the student's current activity, get his full attention, and send a message to him that you expect him to attend to what you're saying. In short, eye contact helps you communicate that you mean business.

The Command

Once you obtain eye contact, it's time to issue the command. There are many ways of issuing a command, and no particular strategy works for everyone. The exact way anyone issues a command is a matter of that person's personality and therefore is very individual. However, there are several principles that are crucial to increasing the effectiveness of a command. Keeping them in mind will help you increase your student's compliance.

Eye Contact

First, remember to issue the command *while* you are looking your student right in the eyes. Don't look away until you finish telling your student the command. If your student briefly looked at you and then looked away, do not be concerned, and do not attempt to get eye contact again. You have already accomplished what the eye contact was intended to do. Now, proceed to the command itself.

Be Respectful but Firm

Both components of this statement are equally important. The respectful part is crucial. Think about your own life and people you've known who were in positions of authority over you. You probably remember some of them more fondly than others. Those you still remember kindly were respectful of you and addressed you with consideration. On the other hand, those you disliked the most were the ones that made you feel unimportant and treated you as if you were inferior. You were probably more likely to follow a command given by a "nice" boss than a "nasty" one. It is true that we respect those who respect us.

When I hold training workshops, one of the most frequent laments I hear from teachers is that their students don't respect them, yet I encounter so many teachers that command their students with an angry voice, and sometimes with demeaning remarks. Teachers who want respect from their students must first give it. Students deserve to be treated with dignity.

Having said that, remember that the command must also be stated firmly. Some teachers give commands to students in a plaintive manner, almost as if they were begging for obedience. Others explain a command excessively, almost as if they were asking the student to agree that the command was a good idea. Still others preface a command by saying, "Do me a favor. . . ." All teachers have probably done these things from time to time, and with some students these approaches may work well. An impulsive or oppositional student, however, will interpret these situations differently and quickly jump to a perception that compliance is optional. Obviously, you don't mean it this way.

Likewise, teachers often ask a student to do something by starting with, "Would you please. . . ." Again, this isn't a good idea, because this form of a question can be answered very easily by saying "no." An oppositional student may say "no" anyway, but don't set up the situation in a way that makes it easier for her to do so. Instead, say what you mean in a manner that commands attention. Instead of asking, *tell* your student in a respectful but firm voice what you want her to do. Speak deliberately and clearly, with a tone that commands attention, but without yelling.

To summarize, approach your student so that eye contact is possible; call his name or ask him to look at you, and while looking at him, state an instruction to perform a concrete action (e.g., "Please put this away now").

Nonverbal Language

Your nonverbal communication must also be commanding. Nonverbal communication includes body posture, hand gestures, facial expression, the tone of your voice, and the manner in which you speak (e.g., how rapid your speech is or whether your voice goes up and down or breaks while you speak). Generally, take a commanding posture (standing may help), and keep your hands next to your body. Don't grimace; show a deliberate facial expression. Use a firm tone in your voice (it may help to raise your voice very slightly, but do not yell), and produce words in a calculated, deliberate manner.

The younger the student is, the more important it is for you to pay attention to nonverbal language, because her ability to reason with words and respond to verbal communication is still developing. Think about a child at age three or four months. When addressed by a parent, she probably already responded to feelings and expressions, even though she had little ability to understand words and phrases. The way she was able to receive the messages was through the expression on parent's face, the body posture, and the voice intonation.

In fact, a young child's ability to recognize facial expressions is universal, and you may recall some of the research on this topic that is presented in Introduction to Psychology college courses. Many studies have been performed in which infants were presented with pictures (or videos) of faces with various emotions on them. The same person was always shown but each time with a different facial expression of emotion. The infants correctly recognized each emotion and exhibited responses appropriate to each emotion (e.g., they laughed when it was a happy face and cried or withdrew when the face was sad or angry). Moreover, when the images of the human face with different emotions were shown to infants from different cultures, the results were similar.

Young students pay less attention to your words and respond mostly to the nonverbal messages you convey with your body, your face, and the tone of your voice. The older the student, the more he focuses on the verbal message, but he'll remain tuned-in to your nonverbal language as well. If your words say one thing (e.g., "I want compliance"), but your nonverbal communication sends another message (e.g., "I'm not sure if this is going to work"), the student will pick up on your hesitancy, and the likelihood of compliance will diminish.

As teacher, you must remember that nonverbal communication cannot be faked. It reflects your true feelings, regardless of whether you are consciously aware of them. If you are hesitant, you student will perceive this, even if you try to convey that you are decisive and firm. Don't merely *try* to convince yourself that the approach you are following will work, *do* convince yourself that it will work. Have confidence that you'll make it work. As discussed in the previous chapter, if you prepare yourself by expecting realistic outcomes, understanding that your job as a teacher is to stay in control and administer consequences, and remaining calm, you truly will believe that what you do will work, and your nonverbal language will convey that message to your student. That's when she'll recognize that you really mean business.

On the other hand, although you must adopt a commanding posture, avoid violating your student's space if possible. Human beings, regardless of age, become uncomfortable when their space is violated. In an interaction in which you are commanding your student to perform an action, the situation may become more tense, and violating your student's space can agitate him further. Of course, eye contact is important, so get close to your student but do not make him feel that you are trying to intimidate him physically to get your way.

Do Not Negotiate or Argue

As part of your firm approach, be prepared to fend off your student's protests and attempts at negotiations. Don't bargain with your student, and don't debate your point. Don't continue to explain why you want him to perform the action you commanded. Generally, it's OK to give your student one reason, briefly and to the point, but don't overexplain. If your student continues to ask, it's OK to say, "I already explained it to you," or "Because I said so." Remember, you're not asking your student to approve what you commanded.

Watching teachers interact with students, I sometimes get the impression that teachers want to convince their students that what they are asking is the right thing to do, in the hope that the students will then agree to do it. This is inappropriate. First, it isn't your student's place to judge what you tell her to do. Second, it isn't your place to convince her of the appropriateness of your command or to make excuses about why you want something done. Can you imagine a boss doing this with an employee or a superior officer in the armed forces asking the subordinates to accept a direct command? In this way, the teacher-student relationship is a superior-subordinate relationship.

In summary, if your student questions your command, give a brief explanation only *once,* or state, "Because I said so," and do not respond to all further protests or questions.

One Thing at a Time

Your command should include only one action that you want your student to perform. This is very important—only one item at a time. If you want your student to perform several actions, command him to do the first and then issue another command after the first action is completed. This, again, has implications for compliance. It's much easier for your student to ignore or defy a command that calls for multiple actions (a so-called "chain command") than a command that calls for just a single action. Think about those students that have attentional difficulties. At best, they'll focus on just the first or last command; at worst, they'll ignore all of them altogether—and telling a very young student to do more than one thing at a time surely spells trouble.

Ask Your Student to Repeat the Command

Finally, you may want to ask your student to repeat the command back to you. This isn't essential, but it may be very helpful if your student has attentional problems or if you're unsure whether he truly processed what you said. Those students who get too engrossed in activities and find it hard to stop them will be forced not only to attend to what you say (when you seek the eye contact) but also to repeat it back to you. This interrupts what they were doing and increases their ability to process what you commanded.

Here is a summary of what we covered thus far:

- Approach your student and look at her.
- Call your student's name or ask her to look at you.
- State a specific command in a firm voice, such as, "Please put this away now," or "Please return to your seat."
- If your student asks you why, give a brief explanation such as, "Because we have to move on to another subject," or "Because play time is over," and respond to all further questions by ignoring them or stating, "I already told you why," or "Because I said so."

- After you state your command, you may want to ask your student to repeat the command to you by saying, "Please repeat what I just told you to do." Correct any inaccuracies and state, "Yes, please do it now."

The Follow-Up Look

Once you've issued the command, you must do one more thing: absolutely . . . nothing! That is, nothing except stand and look at your student for an additional 15 seconds or so. Don't move. To time yourself, count (silently) from 101 to about 115 or 120. This may seem strange at first, but think about what this will accomplish. It will create some tension in the situation that will encourage your student to process what you said. Teachers understand that sometimes they need to increase pressure on their students to obtain compliance, but they often pressure students through yelling or becoming disrespectful and demeaning. These methods escalate conflict and lead to altercations. Standing and silently looking at the student will put pressure on him without escalating conflict.

Think about your own experiences: Have you ever had anyone stand and look at you after you were told to do something? Do you remember how uncomfortable you felt? If you can't relate to this point, do an experiment. Ask your spouse or a friend to ask you spontaneously to do something and then to stand and look at you until you do it. I'm sure that you'll experience the feeling of pressure. That is exactly what you want to convey to your student, and doing so through just standing and looking at her is humane and effective.

If your student asks why you're looking at her, you can respond in several ways. Ignore the question, tell her you're looking because she still hasn't done what you asked her to do, or say that you are doing so because you want to. Remember, however, that you don't owe your student an explanation. Most students will want to do what you asked just to get you off their back, and that's a good beginning.

While looking at your student, avoid responding to what she may say. She may impulsively start to protest when you first issue the command and may at first say "no," but when she sees that you aren't going away and that you're not going to let up, she'll feel the pressure you are putting on her and start to comply. I have witnessed this classic example many times: When asked to start picking up, a student at first says, "No, I'm not finished," but when the teacher continues to stand there and look at her, the student starts picking up, all the while saying, "I don't want to," or "I'm not finished." The teacher in this situation didn't need to respond to anything that the student said because, even though she protested all the way, she obeyed the command.

Positive Feedback

If your student complied with your command, you must show him your appreciation of his cooperation. This is accomplished through positive feedback. As a teacher, one of your primary goals is to help him recognize what consequences results from his behavior. These consequences should be as immediate as possible, because it will improve his ability to recognize the connection between his behavior and the resulting consequence. When your student makes the right choice and performs what you asked, he needs to receive an immediate positive consequence, and when he doesn't, an immediate negative consequence should follow. Negative consequences are addressed later in this book. For now, I'll focus on the positive consequences.

Every time your student obeys you, give him a sign of your appreciation and approval. There are several ways to give positive feedback. Verbal ways to do so include saying things such as "Thank you," "Great job!" "Cool!" "Way to go," "I like it when you do what I ask," and "I really appreciate it when you listen to me." These are even more effective when supplemented by nonverbal signs of approval (e.g., a smile, a wink, or a gentle pat on the shoulder). Remember, however, that although children are very sensitive to nonverbal messages, some students, particularly younger ones or those with attentional problems, may not make the connection that your wink or smile is in direct response to the behavior. Consequently, try to make sure that you always use both verbal and nonverbal means and you'll more effectively drive the point home. This will make your student feel good, and he'll want to feel this way again in the future. If he makes the connection that doing what you asked resulted in a consequence that made him feel good, it is more likely that he'll want to repeat this behavior in the future.

Keep in mind that students who frequently are oppositional and defiant are not used to receiving positive feedback. Instead, they experience frequent conflicts with their teachers, parents, and caretakers, usually many times per day. After a while, they grow to expect screaming, yelling, and being scolded and punished. Conversely, they don't expect praise, and at first they may not recognize why you are being nice to them. If they receive positive feedback so infrequently, they may not know how to react. I have worked with many parents and teachers who, after initiating my techniques, reported to me that their children or students didn't know how to handle praise and, at first, became uncomfortable. I have also observed this firsthand when watching interactions between parents and children, or teachers and students. It may take some time before your student feels comfortable with hearing good things said about him and his behavior. You'll need to offer frequent and consistent praise before your student makes the connection between his behavior and your praise and starts to expect that doing what you ask will make him feel good in return. One final point needs to be emphasized: Avoid the so-called back-handed compliments, in which you acknowledge positive behavior on the one hand ("that was good") but reprimand at the same time ("but next time, do it right when I ask"). As you help your student experience that a compliment feels good, you don't want to minimize that positive feelings by including any negative content.

Let's re-examine the example we provided at the beginning of this chapter, but this time let's think about what it may look like if the teacher utilized the techniques described in this chapter.

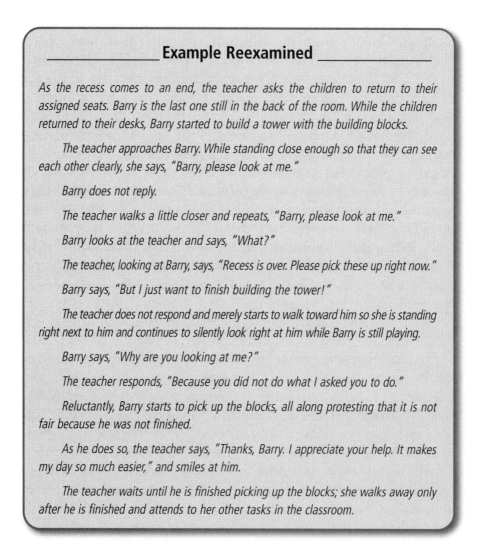

_____ Example Reexamined _____

As the recess comes to an end, the teacher asks the children to return to their assigned seats. Barry is the last one still in the back of the room. While the children returned to their desks, Barry started to build a tower with the building blocks.

The teacher approaches Barry. While standing close enough so that they can see each other clearly, she says, "Barry, please look at me."

Barry does not reply.

The teacher walks a little closer and repeats, "Barry, please look at me."

Barry looks at the teacher and says, "What?"

The teacher, looking at Barry, says, "Recess is over. Please pick these up right now."

Barry says, "But I just want to finish building the tower!"

The teacher does not respond and merely starts to walk toward him so she is standing right next to him and continues to silently look right at him while Barry is still playing.

Barry says, "Why are you looking at me?"

The teacher responds, "Because you did not do what I asked you to do."

Reluctantly, Barry starts to pick up the blocks, all along protesting that it is not fair because he was not finished.

As he does so, the teacher says, "Thanks, Barry. I appreciate your help. It makes my day so much easier," and smiles at him.

The teacher waits until he is finished picking up the blocks; she walks away only after he is finished and attends to her other tasks in the classroom.

> *If Barry is picking up too slowly or tries to continue building while he is picking up, the teacher says, "Here, let's do it together. You have to do it with me." She assists in the cleanup and still offers praise when it is done.*
>
> • • •

This example shows an interaction that resulted in compliance. What if it did not work? That is discussed in the next chapter. Notice that the teacher did not force a confrontation and was willing to start the cleanup with the student to help him along. Teachers can expect that this technique will result in compliance, although not always. Nevertheless, this technique includes components of communication with oppositional students that must be maintained while we cover future steps. Please practice this approach repeatedly until it becomes so automatic that you no longer need to consciously think about using all three components (attentional cue, a single-action command stated in the affirmative, a follow-up look) of an effective command.

Using This Technique With Adolescents

The command-giving procedure described in this chapter is effective with students of all ages. However, the older the student, the more important it is to slightly modify some of the components.

The Attentional Cue

As with younger students, it is important to preface the command with a cue. All the reasons explained previously still apply to adolescents: the need to prepare their brain that a communication is about to be issued, the need to interrupt whatever they are doing so they process the command more fully, and the need to personalize the interaction so that it becomes a person-to-person exchange.

As with younger students, the best way to get the student's attention is to call his name. However, teachers of teenage students should be careful not to get into conflict over whether the student will look at the teacher. Generally, as long as the teacher gets the impression that the student heard the cue, interrupted what he was doing and is in a listening mode (even if no actual eye contact takes place), the teacher accomplished the goals of this technique. If the student responded but still appears to be doing something while he is listening, the teacher may politely say, "Please stop what you are doing for a moment because I would like to tell you something." Usually, that is sufficient for the student to be ready to listen to what is about to be said.

The Command

Older students usually exhibit more sophisticated reasoning abilities that lead teachers to believe that they are able to process and follow more complex commands. In some instances, that may be the case. However, many adolescents still exhibit difficulties processing instructions, especially when they are being told something they do not really want to hear. Thus, it is important that teachers remember that, although an older student is capable of more complex reasoning skills, command giving should still be stated in the affirmative and should still contain a request to perform a single, specific action.

Teachers must also keep in mind that students who are entering their teenage years are now beginning to grapple with the concept of control, especially trying to prove to themselves how much control over their environment they really exert. It is very common for students in that developmental period to challenge authority. Thus, the more they feel that they are being bossed around, the more they may respond with an oppositional attitude.

It is still important, however, for teachers to act with authority. A teacher of adolescents must strike a balance. On the one hand, commands should be issued calmly and should be prefaced with "please," so that students do not feel that the teacher is being inappropriately commanding, bossy, and disrespectful. On the other hand, the teacher should be firm and state the command as a simple, straightforward request (not a question). Again, it is important to state a clear, specific action that should be performed now. Addressing more complex situations, in which students are expected to comply with multistep requirements (e.g., completing work) are discussed later in the book.

The Follow-Up Look

As with younger students, it is important to send the message to the student that he is expected to do what was asked of him. The follow-up look is an effective way to do so. In some cases, using the same technique previously described for younger students may be effective. However, some older students may have a negative response when the teacher continues to look at them. They may feel that the look is a form of a stare and may then try to prove to the teacher that they will not allow themselves to be stared down. Such a contest of stares is not productive.

Instead, teachers should be sensitive to the student's reaction to the follow-up look. If she seems to respond negatively to being looked at and tries to get into a staring match, the teacher should look away but remain in the vicinity of the student. By continuing to be close to the student, the teacher will accomplish nearly the same effect as with the look: She will still feel the teacher's presence and therefore will find it more difficult to merely continue with her current activity. The teacher is still applying the pressure discussed earlier but in a manner that feels less like a challenge.

• Putting It All Together •

When you utilize the approach described in this chapter, you begin to put more pressure on your students to obey than you probably have in the past. This step alone may work to increase the rate of your students' compliance with your commands. If this procedure doesn't immediately seem to work, don't stop. Although it may take some time, and evidence of progress may be gradual, it is an effective technique. The approach discussed in this chapter provides a foundation upon which further interventions described in this book are built. To start, focus only on giving effective commands and administering positive feedback whenever you get compliance. For now, when you do not get compliance, respond as you usually would in such a situation.

You may ask, "How long do I have to keep using this step?" Some techniques should be utilized on an ongoing basis, and Step 1 falls into this category. It is desirable for it to become automatic so that you no longer have to actively think about it when you issue daily commands.

With teenagers, remember to modify this approach to avoid getting into staring contests. Teenagers exert themselves by challenging authority in an attempt to figure out how much control they have over their own life and destiny. Being stared at may cause your student to stare back in an attempt to win this contest of wills. Instead, obtain initial eye contact (or, at least, make sure you have your student's attention), but instead of continuing to look right at him after you issued the command, stay in the vicinity to communicate to him that he isn't off the hook until you obtain compliance.

Before you proceed further, practice this step for at least one to two weeks. Step 2, described in the next chapter, builds upon Step 1 and helps you address situations in which Step 1 did not produce compliance.

Step 1 Checklist

Give Effective Commands

Preparation

Realistic Expectations

No student obeys 100% of the time, and oppositional students have more problems with following directions and commands. They are often impulsive; consequently, they are defiant. No approach will result in eliminating all compliance problems, but specific techniques can help.

Why Do Students Behave the Way They Do?

Students don't misbehave just to get you mad or to get back at you. They misbehave because they can't follow the command; they don't know how to do what the teachers ask; they see no reason why they should obey; or they can get what they want by not listening.

Remember, students' behaviors are goal directed: They use whatever means they know to get what they want.

Personality Factors

A strong-willed child will grow up to be a tenacious adult. A strong personality is an asset in life; the goal of teaching is not to break the strong will but to help the student develop appropriate judgment and self-control.

Procedure

1. Attentional Cue
   - ❏ Call your student's name.
   - ❏ Get eye contact; do not give long-distance commands.
   - ❏ For teenagers, get a sense that they are listening and have interrupted the current activity, even if you do not get direct eye contact.

2. Command
   - ❏ Address your student in a respectful but firm manner.
   - ❏ Stand with a commanding posture but try not to violate the student's space.
   - ❏ Speak deliberately and clearly with a commanding tone, but do not yell. Don't ask your student to do you a favor; you don't mean that. Just state, calmly but firmly, what you want him to do.
   - ❏ State only one item that you want him to do. If necessary, issue a follow-up command after the initial action is completed.
   - ❏ Don't debate or overexplain (maximum of one brief explanation). Don't bargain with your student.
   - ❏ It may be helpful to ask your student to repeat the command, but do not create a conflict about whether the student will do so (especially when applying this technique with teenagers).

3. Follow-Up Look
   - ❏ Stand and look at the student for about 15 seconds.
   - ❏ With teenagers, instead of looking right at the student, you may want to look in another direction but remain in the student's close proximity.

If your student obeys the command, make sure to give verbal and nonverbal praise.

Step 2

Give Effective Warnings

How successful were you in implementing Step 1? Most teachers find that Step 1, by itself, produces some compliance but does not work all the time. If you have seen no improvement, it may mean that you are not using some of the techniques discussed in the previous chapter consistently. Perhaps you did not remember to issue the attentional cue, or you did not state a single, clear, and deliberate command. How about the follow-up look? Many teachers find that technique very awkward and need time to become comfortable with it. Don't be surprised if you fall back into your old habits on a regular basis. You may need to give yourself more time before proceeding to Step 2.

If you are consistently using all techniques described in the previous chapter, and the difference is not significant, you are probably dealing with a student who presents with difficulties that cannot be remedied just by using Step 1 alone (as is often the case). Don't give up. Continue to use Step 1, and add Step 2 to further build on that foundation.

In most cases, when Step 1 doesn't result in compliance, several important factors affect the interaction.

Noncompliant Interaction

An interaction between a person in charge (e.g., a teacher) and a subordinate (e.g., a student) that results in noncompliance is recognized as one of the most frequent trouble spots in behavior management. It has become known in the psychological literature as a *noncompliant interaction.* As described by Russell Barkley (1997) in his book *Defiant Children,* the noncompliant interaction involves repetition loops that escalate the situation. When a student does not comply with a command, a teacher usually repeats the command. Each repetition does not produce compliance, and with each reiteration the teacher feels more frustrated. You know the pattern. When you tell your student, "Put this away," and your student ignores you or keeps saying "In a minute," your frustration increases, your voice rises, and before you know it, you're upset and you don't know what to do.

When your level of frustration reaches a boiling point, you may start threatening, but because you already feel angry, you likely threaten with consequences that are not immediately available ("If you keep doing this, you will not like your report card!") or not realistic ("If you don't put it away, I will not let you play with it ever again!") or consequences that you may not often administer ("If you don't stop, I am calling your mother!"). Your student perceives the low likelihood of your follow-through and recognizes that you are only trying to scare him. Consequently, this scare tactic is rarely effective. Interactions such as these usually result in the teacher backing off and giving up on seeking compliance or sending the student out of the classroom (e.g., to see the principal). Neither of these is a desirable outcome, especially on a regular basis.

Here is a portion of the example examined in the previous chapter.

Example

As the recess comes to an end, the teacher asks the children to return to their assigned seats. Barry is the last one still in the back of the room. While the children return to their desks, Barry starts to build a tower with the building blocks.

The teacher addresses Barry from across the classroom: "Barry, put those away and return to your seat."

Barry replies, "In a minute."

The teacher starts giving out a handout with a math assignment. Barry is still playing with the blocks. The teacher says, "Barry, I said put those away and come back to your desk."

"But I just want to finish building the tower!" Barry says.

The other children start working, and the teacher starts to circulate around the room to see if anyone needs help. Barry is still playing.

She raises her voice: "Barry, your work is waiting here for you." He responds, "I'm not finished!"

The teacher answers a question from another student and realizes that Barry is still in the back of the room. She tells Barry, "Come to your desk now, or I'll have to tell your mother you're not listening."

Barry does not respond. The teacher, still in the front of the room, answers another student's question and then yells, "Barry, did you hear me? I am calling your mother!"

Barry does not respond and continues to build.

The teacher, now visibly angry, marches toward Barry, starts to take the blocks out of his hands, and pulls him toward his desk. Barry starts yelling and crying: "But I was not finished! It's not fair!" He throws the blocks he still has in his hand across the room.

He gets to his desk, still crying, and his noise is disrupting the other students in the classroom.

— • • • —

The situation with Barry clearly followed the pattern described here. As in the previous chapter, there were problems at the very onset of the interaction, when the teacher started to seek compliance. When the commands were not effective, Barry and his teacher entered a repetition loop as she repeated her command several times. Each repetition failed to produce compliance, resulting only in the increase of the teacher's frustration. She continued to repeat the command, but each repetition was no more effective. Along the way, she became angrier. The more she repeated herself, the more she recognized that she was ineffective. In addition, the more frustrated she became, the less likely Barry was to comply.

This continued until she felt that she had to do something else, and she entered the second repetition loop when she attempted to bluff Barry with whatever she thought sounded scary. However, this also proved ineffective. Why didn't it work? Barry's teacher surely must have used this (or a similar) threat in the past and didn't follow through with it. Why should Barry expect her to follow through this time? Additionally, Barry was already getting angrier, and his ability to utilize self-control was diminishing with the escalation. Thus, the longer the interaction continued, the less likely Barry was to make the right choice. In the end, the scare tactic was ineffective and only caused the teacher to become even more frustrated.

When the last-ditch effort failed, the teacher felt that she had to force compliance with any reasonable means available to her, and she physically forced the student to do what she originally commanded. This approach, although temporarily effective in ending the current exchange, doesn't produce beneficial results in the long term, and the student is no more likely to be compliant in the future. On the contrary, being physically forced to comply makes many students feel invaded upon and negatively affects their relationship with the teacher. In turn, the student is even less likely to listen to that teacher in the future.

On the other hand, a teacher may instead acquiesce and perform the stated task herself. In a choice between aggression or acquiescence, the latter is probably the better choice, but it teaches the student that if she does not comply, the teacher will simply perform the task for her. Ultimately, neither aggression nor acquiescence is desirable; neither produces compliance, and more important, neither carries immediate consequences for the student. Thus, either way, the situation will not teach the student about the consequences of her behavior.

How do we break the chain of events and turn a noncompliant interaction into a compliant one? A compliant interaction must start with the successful implementation of the techniques in Step 1, which help the teacher issue a command that is more likely to be obeyed the first time around (attentional cue, single command stated in the affirmative, a follow-up look)—but what if that doesn't work? How do we avoid the repetition loops that escalate conflict and further reduce the likelihood that the interaction will have a positive outcome?

Compliant Interaction

Researchers and clinicians, especially Russell Barkley (1997), developed a technique that helps eliminate the repetition loops. My own research with two groups of teachers confirmed that this technique is also effective with students (Kapalka, 2005a, 2007a). It is OK to repeat a command to your student, but there's a way to do it that minimizes escalation and conflict and maximizes the likelihood of compliance.

Start With Fully Implemented Step 1

Before you repeat a command, make sure that you have utilized all of the techniques discussed in Step 1 (thus, once again, you are advised to practice Step 1 by itself long enough so that you are comfortable and consistent with using it). For example, make sure that you don't repeat the command until after you've looked silently at your student for about 15 seconds. This may feel like a long time, but resist the temptation and do *not* repeat the command until after that time has passed. If you allow enough time to put silent pressure on your student, you may not need to repeat the command.

Repeat Step 1

If you did allow the recommended time and your student still didn't comply, repeat the entire procedure described in Step 1. Repeat the attentional cue and then say, "I said . . ." and state the command again. Then, stand and look at your student for another 15 seconds. In essence, you are repeating exactly what you did in the entire Step 1 procedure, but this time you reintroduce your command by telling your student, "I said . . . ," and you may raise your voice *slightly* (be careful not to yell) to convey to your student that you mean business and you won't just go away and forget about it if he does not listen.

By repeating yourself only once, you are eliminating the repetition loop. You are thus eliminating the process by which you work yourself up and get increasingly frustrated with each repetition of your command. Instead, because you'll be able to remain calmer, you'll be able to think more clearly, and this will make a significant difference in what is about to follow.

If, after you've repeated yourself once (and allowed time for another extended look), your student still doesn't obey, do not repeat the command again. Further repetitions are not likely to work. Instead, calmly communicate to your student that you are ready to raise the stakes. You will do so by issuing a warning or an ultimatum.

The Warning

Notice that when I analyze Barry's interaction with his teacher in the aforementioned example, I refer to the teacher's ultimatum as a threat, a scare tactic. Here, I am advising the use of a warning. What is the difference? A threat is issued in desperation because we do not know what else to do. We want to "scare" someone into compliance. When frustrated, we issue a threat because we want the recipient to think, "Oh my gosh, not *that*!!" and do what we command to avoid experiencing this ominous outcome.

Instead, a warning is an announcement of a consequence. Rather than make something appear scarier (desperately hoping that it will have more impact), a warning accurately and calmly portrays a choice of outcomes. Because it does not sound scary, it sounds more believable. Because it does not threaten, it minimizes further escalation. In the end, all of these factors increase the likelihood of its effectiveness.

First, think of your options. You're still relatively calm, because you have not been repeating yourself and getting frustrated by the noncompliance. Because you are calmer, you can think more clearly and will be able to find a consequence for your student that will be realistic, and you'll be more likely to follow through with it. Not only will your student recognize your determination, but he'll also recognize that you are warning him of an action that isn't a hollow threat and that you're likely to do what you state. Because he will also be calmer, he'll be more able to consider the options and make an informed choice of behavior.

Select an appropriate consequence (I provide some suggestions in the next section) and give your student a warning. It should follow all the components of an effective command described in Step 1 (attentional cue, single statement expressed in the affirmative, a follow-up look). Issue the attentional cue, and then say "if you do not . . . , then . . . ," and again administer the follow-up look for about 15 seconds.

Let's review what we've covered thus far.

- First, perform the complete sequence involved in Step 1 (see the previous chapter):
  o Position yourself so that you can see your student.
  o Call your student's name or ask her to look at you.
  o State a specific command in a firm voice, such as "Please start picking up now," or "Please take out your math book."
  o Continue to look at her for about 15 seconds.
- If your student obeys, give praise (verbal and nonverbal).
- If your student does not obey, maintain visual contact and repeat the complete sequence in Step 1:
  o Again, call your student's name or ask her to look at you.
  o State, "I said, please start picking up now," or "I said, please open the math book."
  o Continue to look at her for about 15 seconds.
- If your student obeys, give praise (verbal and nonverbal).
- If your student does not obey, administer the warning, using the same sequence of techniques as in Step 1:
  o Again, call your student's name or ask her to look at you.
  o State, "If you do not start picking up now, I will do it for you, but you will not play with them for the rest of the week," or "If you do not open the math book now, I will write a note to your mom that you did not want to do your math today."
  o Continue to look at her for about 15 seconds.
- If your student obeys, give praise (verbal and nonverbal). If not, calmly administer the stated consequence.

If you need to administer the consequence, do it quickly. The more immediate the consequence, the more effective it will be. It's a teaching tool. Your student must make the connection between the behavior and the consequence. The more quickly you administer it, the more likely your student is to learn from it. Administer the consequence calmly but firmly and swiftly. Sometimes you may need to use a consequence that cannot be administered until later (e.g., having the student miss recess). If this is the case, state the consequence immediately and be sure to follow through in administering it at the appropriate time.

One final point: Never repeat a warning. Your student must learn that, when the warning is issued, the next thing that will happen if he doesn't comply is the administration of the stated consequence. If the warning is repeated, the student will start to catch on that the teacher would really prefer not to administer the warning. With each repetition, the warning becomes less effective. So, once again, do not ever repeat a warning—just do what you said you will do if noncompliance continues.

Examples of appropriate consequences for noncompliance include the following:

- Having toys put away for a day or a few days
- Removing computer privileges for the rest of the day
- Being excluded from a game during recess
- Being excluded from recess altogether
- Having a note written to the student's parents (e.g., in a journal, as described in a later step)
- Being placed in time-out (as discussed in the next chapter)

As you see, it isn't necessary to intimidate students with extreme consequences. The consequences listed here do not sound scary; therefore, students will easily see that you are likely to do what you warn. Be prepared that students will have to experience these consequences before they recognize that, although they are not scary, they do result in the loss of a privilege or a similar event. Although administering them one time may not be enough to teach a student to heed the warning, consistency is likely to result in gradual improvement.

You will notice that these examples include consequences that are rather minor (e.g., being excluded from a game) and others that are more significant (e.g., missing recess). Teachers should keep a hierarchy in mind and try to use primarily those consequences that are less severe. The more severe the consequences, the fewer remain available to administer repeatedly. In other words, if you administer the more severe consequences too quickly, you will rapidly run out of options for the rest of the school day.

Students need repeated trials to help them learn. The more impulsive the student, the less likely she is to learn from any one instance. Thus, having enough consequences to use throughout a school day will help her repeatedly experience a situation and its outcome, thus increasing the likelihood of her learning. Gradually, she will start to anticipate the consequence, and that is when you will notice a significant improvement in compliance.

What about those students who don't seem to respond to negative consequences? When I work with teachers, many of them express that they have tried all different types of punishments with their students and none have worked. In my experience, however, students who don't respond to negative consequences are truly rare. More commonly, I encounter teachers who have tried negative consequences, but the student seemingly did not respond; on closer scrutiny, however, the consequences were not administered consistently. In other words, although the student was often threatened with a consequence for noncompliance (e.g., "No computer for the rest of the day"), the teacher either did not follow through consistently or allowed the student to earn the lost privilege back later in the day. Therefore, the student did not experience that every warning consistently resulted in the stated consequence. Also, teachers sometimes do not allow for sufficient time and opportunity for repetition for the consequences to really teach the student about the outcome of his behavior. They administered a consequence once or twice, and on the third occasion, when a warning did not produce compliance, they concluded that the student did not care about being punished and so this approach would not work. Instead, teachers must keep in mind that students have to experience the consequence many times (at least five or six times, maybe more) before they make the connection that a warning really does announce an undesired consequence for noncompliance.

Please also be aware that Step 2 may not produce the desired results the first, third, or even the fifth time you administer it. That doesn't mean that it won't work. Impulsive and oppositional students are known to have difficulties learning from experience. Some students may learn after being exposed to a consequence once or twice, but impulsive and oppositional students are likely to need that exposure six or eight times. It doesn't mean that the consequence won't work, only that the student needs more time to learn the lesson. Often, these are the students about whom teachers say that the consequences don't work. The truth is, the teachers haven't persevered long enough to give the consequences enough time to work.

Keep in mind that your goal is not to get compliance at any price but to administer consequences, both positive and negative, following the student's behavior. Each interaction with your student should be a learning experience for her about how the world will respond to her behaviors.

As much as possible, avoid administering any consequences that weren't mentioned in your warning. Consequences are much more effective if the student first hears an announcement of a consequence and makes a decision about whether to heed the warning. The ultimate goal of this program is to help students improve their self-control. Self-control involves the ability to stop and think about a consequence that may take place and to decide whether the outcome is desirable. It is that processing that we strive to improve, and it takes place when the student is cued that a consequence is likely to occur. Without such a warning, when the consequence is a surprise, this form of processing does not occur, so consequences that were not announced before are not nearly as effective. True, you may feel that the student should have expected the consequence even without your explicit warning. That may be the case for many students, but remember that you are dealing with a student who is impulsive and does not stop to think about what will occur. The most effective way to improve that is to help him think about possible consequences before they are administered.

When Your Student Changes Her Mind

If, after you've administered the consequence, your student then changes her mind and now wants to perform the desired behavior, don't let her do it. Tell her, "It's too late now. Next time, do what I ask when I ask you to do it." Continue to administer the consequence you selected, and don't change your mind.

Praise

Here is one final but very important point: If, during this procedure (but before the negative consequence had to be administered), your student obeys the command, remember to give him praise. Don't give any less praise if your student obeys you after the repetition of the command (or even after the warning) than you would have had he listened the first time you said it. Helping your student learn to listen on the first try is discussed in another chapter.

Once again, when issuing praise, avoid backhanded compliments ("You did that so well, but why couldn't you do it the first time I asked?"). Don't even mention that it took a warning to get the compliance. The fact is, you got the compliance, so give your student praise and make her feel good about obeying you.

Let's reexamine the example we provided at the beginning of this chapter, but this time let's think about what it may look like if the teacher utilized the techniques described in this chapter. Notice that the following example illustrates the use of Steps 1 and 2 in this situation.

_____ **Example** _____

As the recess comes to an end, the teacher asks the children to return to their assigned seats. Barry is the last one still in the back of the room. While the children return to their desks, Barry starts to build a tower with the building blocks.

The teacher approaches Barry. While standing close enough so that they can both see each other clearly, she says, "Barry, please look at me."

Barry does not reply.

The teacher walks a little closer and repeats, "Barry, please look at me."

Barry looks at the teacher and says, "What?"

The teacher, while looking at Barry, says, "Recess is over. Please pick these up right now."

Barry says, "But I just want to finish building the tower!"

The teacher does not respond and merely starts to walk toward him so she is standing right next to him and continues to silently look right at him while Barry is still playing.

Barry does not respond and continues to build.

The teacher says, "Barry, please look at me."

"What?!" Barry responds.

While looking right at him, the teacher says, "If you do not start picking up these blocks right now, I will do it for you, but you will lose your computer time today."

Barry continues to build, and the teacher continues to look at him. After approximately 15 seconds elapses, the teacher says, "Barry, please look at me."

Barry ignores her.

She bends down and starts picking up the blocks, saying "OK, I see that you have made your choice. I will pick these up, and you will miss your computer time later."

Barry, hurrying, starts to pick up now. The teacher stops Barry and says, "No, it's OK. I'll do it this time. Next time, please do it when I ask."

If Barry starts crying, she escorts him to his desk.

• • •

This example shows an interaction that resulted in noncompliance. What if Barry started to have a tantrum? That is discussed in the next chapter. Notice that, once again, the teacher did not force a confrontation and was willing to clean up the blocks but made sure that he knew that the consequence will take place. It is likely that Barry will need to experience such a consequence several times as he gradually learns to make better decisions.

Using This Technique With Adolescents

As with Step 1, the techniques described in this chapter are effective with students of all ages. However, slight modifications may be needed.

Administer Step 1

In accordance with the suggestions discussed in the previous chapter, administer the attentional cue, but do not get into conflict over whether the student will look at you. Make sure that your student hears the cue, interrupts what she is doing, and is in a listening mode.

Issue one clear, firm command, stated in the affirmative (not in the form of a question). Do not sound "bossy," but make it clear what you expect. Make sure that the command calls for a single, specific action.

Use a follow-up look and give your student time to process the situation before taking any further measures. Avoid a staring match or a power struggle but remain close to the student and make her feel that, unless she does what you asked, the interaction is not over.

Repeat Step 1

It may seem tedious, especially with an older teenager, but do not skip any of the components when you administer the repetition of Step 1. Once again, administer the attentional cue, issue a clear, firm command stated in the affirmative, and administer a version of a follow-up look (while avoiding a power struggle). Make sure that you give the student the required 15 seconds of processing time before you proceed further.

Issue a Warning

Once again, do not skip any of the components when you administer the warning. Start with the attentional cue, issue a clear, firm statement announcing a consequence that will occur as immediately as possible, and do a follow-up look (while avoiding a power struggle). Make sure that you give the student the required 15 seconds of processing time before you proceed further.

Administer a Consequence

If the student complies, praise him and make sure to avoid back-handed comments. Just make him feel good about the good choice he just made.

If he does not comply, clearly but matter-of-factly state what consequence will occur. Make sure that the consequence does not sound vengeful. You do not want the student to feel that you are singling him out. Be prepared that the student is likely to become defensive. Once again, avoid the temptation to become involved in a conflict, even when the student may be appearing to challenge you into one. Remain firm in administering the consequence, but walk away and do not allow the student to engage you in an argument. If he wants to have the last word, so be it. It does not really matter who expresses the last thought. The bottom line is, you will administer the consequence, and so you *will* have the last word, no matter what he says.

If the student becomes disruptive and does not calm down after a moment, administer the techniques discussed in the next chapter.

Putting It All Together

As recommended before, use this procedure as frequently as possible. The more exposure your student has to the sequence described in this chapter, the more learning opportunities she will have to improve her self-control, process the situation, and anticipate the likely consequences of her behavior. Although I have stated this several times before, I repeat here that each stage of Step 2 (administer Step 1, repeat Step 1, administer a warning, issue the appropriate consequence) must be performed, including the three techniques (attentional cue, clear statement in the affirmative, follow-up look) that make up each of those stages. It may seem tedious, but it is absolutely necessary that you do not look for shortcuts or skip any of those components.

If your student starts to throw a tantrum when you administer a negative consequence, ignore it if possible. Most tantrums will not be severe, especially if the interaction did not include a prolonged escalation of mutual frustration, which is so commonly evident in the repetition loops eliminated in this step. If your student becomes physically aggressive or continues exhibiting disruptive behavior for an extended period of time, for now address it in the way you commonly have done thus far. The next step covers how to handle temper tantrums. However, give yourself at least one to two weeks of practicing Step 2 before moving on.

Step 2 Checklist

Give Effective Warnings

Procedure for Compliant Interaction

1. Preparation

❏ Stay calm.
❏ Always stay one step ahead of your student.
❏ Reduce distractions in the classroom.

2. Initial Command

1. Attentional cue

2. Command

3. Follow-up look

3. Repeat Command

❏ Stay calm; don't yell.
❏ Use the same three components given under Initial Command, but raise your voice slightly and say, "I said. . . . "

Note: Repeat the command *one time only!*

o While standing and looking at your student for about 15 seconds after the command, think of a realistic consequence.
o Keep in mind the goal of the consequence: to help your student learn.

4. Warning

❏ Stay calm; *no yelling.*
❏ Use the same three components given earlier, but now inform your student of the consequence: "If you . . . , then. . . ." Remember to use the follow-up look, as you did in Step 1.

5. Consequence

❏ Stay calm.
❏ Administer the consequence (positive or negative).

If your student obeys the command, make sure to give praise.

Step 3

Handle Flare-Ups and Tantrums

By now, you should be following the combined command-giving procedures described in Steps 1 and 2. You should be able to put more pressure on your students in appropriate ways that do not escalate conflict, and you're sending your students a clear message that you mean business. Noncompliance is something you're simply not going to ignore.

Because you're more determined to obtain compliance, your students may react by increasing their protests and outbursts. They probably feel that you mean business and are now under more pressure to do what you expect. For the time being, you may see an increase in temper tantrums. This "fighting-back" response is temporary. Nevertheless, you need to be ready for it and attend to all temper tantrums immediately.

What Is a Temper Tantrum?

Teachers have different ideas about what constitutes a temper outburst. It is important to recognize that some temper outbursts are mild and may not require much action to attend to them. For example, if a student yells out "That's not fair," yet does what you commanded, the mild outburst of emotions is best left alone. If a student doesn't act out while angry but calls you a name, this behavior should not be addressed through the procedures described in this chapter.

Upcoming chapters address these kinds of outbursts and how to handle them.

Let's define a temper tantrum as an encounter during which your student starts to continuously scream, yell, wail, and carry on, and doesn't stop after a short period of time but carries on long enough to disrupt your ability to continue teaching your class. If physical aggression is evident, a temper tantrum includes behaviors that are more significant than, for example, throwing to the floor a pencil that he happened to have in his hand or kicking his desk (but not toppling it) while he is walking away from it. Instead, let's consider temper tantrums as including more serious physical violence, such as throwing something at you, throwing something across the room, turning over a desk, breaking an object, hitting you, or thrashing about in a fit of anger. Those kinds of temper tantrums respond best to the procedures described in this step.

How should you handle those types of outbursts? There are many ways of attending to your students' temper tantrums. Probably the most effective procedure is the time-out. Many of you may say, "I tried time-out, and it didn't work." There are about as many ways to do time-out as there are teachers doing so. You've tried *a* version of time-out, not *the* version of time-out. True, the particular variation you tried may not have worked. In this book, however, you'll find a version of time-out that is specifically fine-tuned to the needs and behaviors of defiant and oppositional students. This particular version may be more likely to work for you than those you may have tried before.

Using Time-Out

Time-out is particularly appropriate as a consequence for temper tantrums. It is a procedure that serves a dual purpose. It acts as a punishment, because it places the student in a spot devoid of stimulation, where she cannot do any of the things she'd like to do, such as interact with others. In this way, one may say that it is punishment by boredom. However, it has another benefit. It also accomplishes the removal of the student from the situation that caused the outburst in the first place. By changing the setting, it helps the student stop the escalation cycle that caused the outburst, because whatever upset her is now eliminated. Although being in time-out may make her angry, at least the situation that caused the initial outburst is temporarily terminated.

Choosing a Time-Out Spot

When you initially decide to implement time-out, you'll first need to select an appropriate time-out spot. The place that you choose must meet several criteria. It must be free of stimulation as much as possible. Your student needs to be isolated in the time-out spot, away from his usual activities (e.g., interacting with students or participating in activities). Many choices are available that meet these criteria: placing a student in a corner in such a way that he is facing away from stimulation, removing him to a hallway (with supervision), or removing him to the office. Depending on your classroom and your student, any of these can work, and you can surely think of many more places where you can place him for time-out.

Before we proceed any further, you must think through some important considerations. First, let's review some legal matters. There are important state-to-state differences in the definition of corporal punishment. Some states define this term very broadly, not only restricting teachers from placing their hands on the students, but also restricting teachers from using certain removal techniques such as placing a student in a corner, facing the wall. In those instances, removal can still be attained by separating the student from others and placing her in a quiet spot, perhaps a corner, but not requiring her to face the wall. It is crucial that teachers check state *and* local district regulations before selecting an intended time-out procedure.

The most effective method of administering time-out is often seen in schools that specialize in teaching students with emotional and behavioral difficulties. These schools often designate special rooms as time-out rooms. These time-out rooms are devoid of stimulation, are often locked (with a teacher or an aide standing outside and looking in to make sure the student is not in danger), and essentially isolate the student for the duration of the time-out. It is clear that this form of time-out requires special circumstances (and often, special permission). However, it is, by far, the most effective. Although teachers in less restrictive settings do not have the option to use such a time-out procedure, this benchmark should be remembered when a time-out procedure within the proper limits of all regulations is established. In other words, teachers should strive to come as close as possible to this "ideal" use of time-out while remaining within the limits of their setting and all appropriate laws and regulations.

First, the place must be as free of stimulation as possible (and practical) to arrange. If you selected a corner in the classroom, make sure that during time-out your student isn't near an area where other students are interacting or performing active tasks (e.g., using the computer). Also, keep other students away as much as possible and redirect them whenever they appear to pay attention to the student in time-out.

Generally, the specific time-out spot should be selected on the basis of whether the student has lost control and continues to act out (scream, yell, kick, etc.). If so, the student should preferably be removed from the classroom into the hallway (with supervision), the front office, or the nurse's office. If the classroom has two teachers, or a teacher and an aide, one can attend to the time-out while the other continues with the rest of the class. If there is only one teacher in the room, such removal-type time-out can still be accomplished. For example, you can give the other students a short assignment to work on independently while you remove the disruptive student into the hallway, accompanying him there to supervise him; or you can alert the front office staff, the nurse, or the vice principal that a student from your room may be sent there and, as long as he is calm, he should be sent back after a specific amount of time. Teachers should experiment with these techniques to come up with the one that will be most effective for each teacher.

If a student acted out and requires time-out but does not continue to be disruptive (e.g., she continues to cry but does not act out physically), such situations are probably best handled by retaining the student in the classroom but separating her from the rest of the students. For example, the student can be placed in the corner of the classroom that is the furthest away from other students and not near a computer, toys, or other items that can attract her attention. Some rearrangement of the classroom may be required to establish such a spot. However, this effort will improve the effectiveness of the time-out and therefore will be rewarded in the long term.

Preparation

Once you select the appropriate spot, more preparation is needed before you attempt your first time-out. Be ready to deal with a lot of resistance during your first time-out intervention. Keep in mind that your student's reaction to the time-out procedure will initially be much stronger than it will be after he gets used to it over time. He'll initially try to pull out all the stops to test whether you'll follow through on what you started. Be ready for it. Don't start the initial time-out encounter and stop it midway through, or your student will feel as though he won and that his behaviors were effective in breaking your attempt at control. Then you'll have a much more difficult time trying it again the next time. So, don't do it until you have selected an appropriate time-out spot and rehearsed it in your mind so you are ready to carry it all the way through, no matter what your student may try to do to stop you. Remember, the first encounter will probably be the worst. Each one after that will become easier as your student gets used to your new attitude, your follow-through, and your readiness to do whatever you need to do to take control of his behavior.

Earlier I began differentiating the types of time-out based on whether physical aggression and continued loss of control is part of your student's temper tantrum. The next section covers what to do if your student is screaming, yelling, and carrying on verbally but is not physically aggressive. Tantrums involving physical aggression and continued loss of control are discussed later in the chapter.

Time-Out for Nonviolent Tantrums

If your student is beginning to work herself up and is carrying on, but has not yet become verbally aggressive or violent, it is best to attempt to warn her about the time-out. Although teachers may find that initially such a warning seems ineffective and time-out nevertheless follows, it is important to persevere with the warning. As the student learns to anticipate the consequence, she will gain self-control, and the warning will gradually become a cue that will help her regain control before the time-out will need to be implemented.

The Warning

Essentially, the warning is administered in accordance with the procedure described in Steps 1 and 2, covered in the previous chapters.

First, issue the attentional cue, and then tell him to stop. Try not to yell, but speak firmly and loudly enough for your student to hear. If at all possible, administer the follow-up look by standing in his vicinity and looking at him for about 15 seconds.

If he continues, issue the attentional cue again, and then warn him by saying, "If you don't stop, you'll have to go to time-out." After the warning, administer the follow-up look (if possible) for about 15 seconds.

The Time-Out Command

If he still doesn't stop, tell him that it's time for time-out. Try to get him to go into the time-out spot on his own, but assist him physically (e.g., by taking his hand) if you must. Place your student in the time-out spot and say, "You have to stay here until I say you can leave." If your student continues to act out while in the time-out spot, say, "If you don't stop, you'll have to stay here longer." If your student attempts to leave, return him to the time-out spot, and repeat the command.

Once your student remains in the time-out spot and begins to calm down, start timing. The amount of time he spends in time-out depends on several factors, particularly your student's age and the seriousness of the offense that got him into the time-out. Generally speaking, one minute per year of age is the rule. Thus, a five-year-old gets a five-minute time-out, a seven-year-old gets a seven-minute one, and so forth. However, some research suggests that shorter time-outs are also effective (Kapalka & Bryk, 2007). I generally recommend that, for students five years old or younger, a two-minute time-out is sufficient, whereas for older students, you may apply the one-minute-per-year-of-age rule.

Remember that your student must be relatively quiet (some crying is OK as long as it is no longer a full-blown tantrum) before you start timing. If you like, you can remind your student, midway through a particularly long acting-out episode during time-out, that his time has not started yet and won't start until he cooperates. Other than that, avoid interacting with your student and don't answer his questions.

It's important that you not tell your student the actual amount of time that he is to stay in time-out. If you set a timer or a stopwatch, do so discreetly for yourself, not for your student. It will be most beneficial when you send him the message that you are the one who decides when he has to go into time-out and when he can leave. This may appear to be a minor point, but you want to remind your student, in obvious and subtle ways, that you are in control of the classroom and that you'll decide his consequences. This reinforces your authority as a teacher—an important component of teaching oppositional and defiant students.

The Release

Once your student has served the time-out sentence, assign a brief task for students to do independently; approach the student in the time-out spot and discreetly ask him, "Do you know why I put you here?" Be calm and don't yell or lecture. Try to get the student to recognize on his own, at least to some extent, the reason why he was placed in time-out. Tell him, "Every time you do this, I'll put you in time-out," and release him from time-out. You want him to learn that you won't tolerate certain behaviors and that these behaviors will lead to the same consequences whenever they occur. If your student is not cooperating with your attempts to get him to own up to the behavior, do not engage in an argument. Stay calm and briefly (without lecturing) tell him why you placed him in time-out and that you'll do it again if the same behavior reoccurs.

After time-out, if possible and practical, it may be helpful to return your student to the same activity that made him act out in the first place. Why? Because, if possible, you want him to be exposed to the very same situation again and have the opportunity to make a better choice of behaviors and experience a different consequence if he makes that better choice. Let's consider the following example: A first-grader was playing with a game and refused to clean up after game time was over. After she serves the required sentence, if she is again required to clean up the game, she now has to handle the same situation. She may indeed make the wrong choice again, and another time-out episode may ensue. However, the more this situation is repeated, the more likely it is that she'll eventually learn to pick up when she is told to do so. In this way, she'll begin to learn how to control herself and to control an impulse to do something that may get her in trouble in the future.

Bear in mind, however, that you must follow through on administering a consequence that you may have already announced before the time-out. For example, let's say that in a situation like that described with the first grader, you initially warned him that, unless he picked up the game, he would not be allowed to play on the computer later that day. Because he did not heed the warning, you proceed to pick up the game pieces yourself and announce that you will administer that consequence (no computer today). If he then has a temper tantrum, time-out will be administered for the temper tantrum, not for the noncompliance. Because you already punished your student for noncompliance, don't try to get him to pick up the game again after the time-out is over. Just finish picking up the game pieces yourself and make sure that you follow through on your stated consequence (no computer today).

To review, the time-out procedure (for nonviolent tantrums) consists of a command to stop, a warning, and the removal into the time-out spot. Once there, your student must be quiet and stay there until you allow her to leave. After serving the minimum sentence, she should be reminded about why she was placed there. Then she can be released to rejoin the classroom activities.

1-2-3 Magic

For very young children, up to about age five or so, the time-out procedure can be modified somewhat. Instead of commanding your student to stop and then warning of impending time-out, you can substitute a 1-2-3 procedure (Phelan, 2003). When your student starts acting out, approach him, look straight into his eyes (if possible), and firmly say, "You have to stop by the time I count to three—this is one" and extend one finger on your hand. Wait about five seconds, while looking right at him. If he continues to act out, say, "This is two" and extend two fingers on your hand. Again, wait about five seconds and keep looking at your student. If he still continues after that interval is over, say, "This is three and now it's time-out" and remove him to the time-out spot. This procedure works very well with young students, especially in situations in which the student is working himself up, becomes too hyperactive, starts running around, and so forth. However, the other procedure, with a command and a warning, also works well for some young students. You may want to try both to see which one feels more comfortable. Remember, however, to select one to use on a continual basis and stick to it consistently.

Time-Out for Violent Tantrums

The procedure described thus far is appropriate to use for nonviolent temper tantrums, but what if your student becomes violent or physically loses control? These tantrums need to be handled similarly, except there should be no command to stop and no warning.

The Time-Out Command

Any violent act (e.g., throwing something at you, throwing something across the room, breaking an object, hitting, or thrashing about in a fit of anger) should lead to the immediate placement of your student in time-out. In this way, the amount of violent behavior will be minimized, and you'll send a strong message to your student that no amount of violence will be tolerated.

As before, tell her that it's time for time-out and try to get her to go into the time-out spot on her own, but assist her physically if you must. Remove the student into the time-out spot (a hallway, a nurse's office, etc.) and say, "You have to stay here until I say (or the nurse says) you can leave." Advise the student that the time-out time will not start until she stops carrying on and becomes quiet.

For violent outbursts, a longer time-out sentence is appropriate. Two minutes per year of age works well with many students. However, this may need to be modified for students age five or younger. For practical reasons, it may be necessary to stay with the shorter, minimum sentence, even for violent tantrums. It may simply be too difficult to keep a five-year-old student, especially an active one, in the time-out spot for 10 minutes. Also, because young children have a limited concept of time, there may be no benefit to a longer time-out; 10 minutes will feel about the same as five minutes to a typical five-year-old student.

Restraint Procedure

Let's discuss the restraint procedure. By *restraint procedure*, I mean a method of maintaining your student in the time-out spot while he continues to be violent. On the other hand, if he isn't being violent but merely tries to get out of the time-out spot before the time is up, your student shouldn't be restrained. Instead, place him back in time-out and tell him to stay there until you say it's OK to leave. You may need to repeat this many times at first, but your student will eventually learn to accept it.

Typical situations that may require a student to be restrained in time-out include kicking, throwing things, getting up off the chair and knocking it over (or throwing it), and hitting the teacher. When any of these acts occur, a restraint procedure should be considered.

Before you implement any restraint procedure, find out whether you have the right, in special circumstances, to place your hands on the student. In nonrestrictive, regular-education settings, teachers usually cannot touch their students during disciplinary methods. These laws were implemented to stop teachers from hitting students. However, the law does not allow you to let the student's behavior place her or other students in danger. Thus, if the student's behavior places her in danger of hurting herself or someone else, most laws and districts allow teachers to physically handle students to restrain them. In more restrictive settings, where students are placed to address their emotional and behavioral problems, permission to restrain students is often given to specially trained teachers. Before restraining your students, be sure that you understand the specifics of your situation and the legal limitations that you must observe.

If you proceed with the restraint, it is best to place your student in a standard chair (not connected to a desk). Place the student on the chair and hold him by the wrists. Get behind him while holding his wrists and carefully bend his arms around both sides of the back rest (one arm on each side) until they are bent behind him at the elbows, around the back rest, with wrists below the student's bottom. It may seem awkward at first, but once you accomplish that, the hold will be comfortable for you and for your student.

There are several reasons why this type of restraint is preferable to the bear-hug procedure that is so popular. First, if the situation has escalated to the point where your student continues to be violent, she may try to hurt you in some way while being restrained. Your student may attempt to bite, kick, or scratch you. The bear hug, unfortunately, makes these easier for her to do. The hold from behind, on the other hand, allows you to stay away from your student's reach, so that she can't kick you or bite you. Once you become skilled at holding your student's wrists firmly with your thumb and index finger of both hands (placed around your student's wrists), you'll see that your student's fingers are too short to reach and scratch you.

Second, the stronger the student, the more strength it takes on the part of the teacher or caretaker to keep holding him in a bear hug. The wrist restraint, on the other hand, will allow you to have significant physical leverage over your student. It takes very little strength to continue to restrain a student in this way, and the hold is very effective in restricting his physical movements.

Finally, a bear hug has a tendency to be very invasive. After all, a large portion of your body comes in contact with a large portion of your student's body. Consequently, a bear hug significantly violates her space, which may agitate her even further. The wrist hold, on the other hand, results in only a small part of your student being held, and because you are behind her, the violation of space is minimal.

While restraining your student, it is important that you calmly say, "If you stop, I'll let go of your hands." Say this in a repetitive manner, in a low, almost chanting, tone of voice. When you feel your student stop squirming, let go of his hands but instruct him to stay put. Be on the alert. Your student may become violent again, and you'll have to quickly reapply the wrist restraint. During the first confrontation, you'll likely have to repeat this several times. Don't be discouraged. Your student will eventually learn that you won't give in and that you won't tolerate violent behavior. Then, future time-out episodes will become shorter and less violent. When your student calms down, start timing the appropriate sentence.

Using This Technique With Adolescents

This is one technique that must significantly be modified for use with teenagers. Time-out can still be used with teens, but it must be administered very differently.

Time-Out Within the Classroom

Administering time-out within the classroom can be difficult with many teenagers. Generally speaking, time-out within the classroom can still be effective, but it is best to administer it while getting the cooperation of the student. In other words, do not make it sound like a punishment. This means that you will have to forgo the warning that is generally useful with younger students. For them, time-out is both a place to calm down and a punishment, so it is appropriate (if violence did not occur) to issue a warning before you administer (and force, if necessary) time-out.

With teenagers, time-out cannot be framed as a punishment. Therefore, no warning should be administered, or a power struggle is likely to ensue, thus clearly communicating to the student the non-voluntary nature of the announced time-out. With most teenagers, this does not work well.

Instead, if you see that a student is getting worked up and escalating her anger, assign a task to the rest of the class, and ask the escalating student to accompany you to the back of the classroom. Ask her to sit down because you briefly want to speak with her. Calmly tell her that it is very difficult for you to teach the class while she is getting louder and that you are asking her to sit in the back for a few minutes so that she can calm down. When she is calmer, explain to her that she can return to her desk.

It is very important that you convey to her that you are doing so because you want to help her calm down. Do not make it sound like a punishment. The more you do, the more resistance you will encounter. Rather, politely but firmly point out that she is getting loud and upset and that this is interfering with your ability to continue teaching. Thus you are taking her to a place where she can have some peace and quiet for a while, and when she feels calmer, she can rejoin the class. The last part is very important. Make sure you point out to your student that it is up to her when she returns to her seat, but you would appreciate that she remain in the back until she feels calm enough to return to her seat and rejoin the classroom.

As discussed earlier in the chapter, it will be beneficial for you to arrange a time-out spot in advance, so you do not have to do it at the time you need to use it. Be sure that the same guidelines apply—a relatively quiet place, in the back of the room, and away from electronics (e.g., a computer) that can easily distract (and occupy) the student.

When I first describe this technique to teachers, many seem initially skeptical. After all, if we make time-out sound optional to the student, will he want to go? Although not every student will comply, and those who do not will have to be handled through removal-type time-out (discussed next), many students actually appreciate the opportunity to be given a spot where they can calm down for a while, as long as it does not appear to them that they are being punished or embarrassed in front of the whole classroom.

Time-Out Outside of the Classroom

When time-out within the classroom is inappropriate (e.g., the student is violent), or when time-out within the classroom is attempted but the student refuses to comply, removal-type time-out has to be administered. Teachers are cautioned to be very careful when approaching teenagers who seem very agitated. Although assaults on teachers are relatively rare, it is sensible for each teacher to be cautious and recognize that many teenagers possess the strength of adults, especially when agitated.

When a student seems agitated, it is very important to avoid performing behaviors that may agitate the student even more (e.g., raising your voice at him, blaming him, questioning him, or violating his space). Instead, it is crucial that you remain calm and address him without appearing agitated yourself.

When a student is behaving in a manner that seems physically intimidating, it is OK to say to the student, "Please stop, you are scaring me." Without embarrassing her, point out to your student that you are not sure whether you have to be afraid that she may want to hurt you. Most students, when agitated, do not recognize how threatening they may appear at the time, and when this is pointed out to them in a manner that is calm and nonconfrontational, they usually become aware that they are acting scary and begin to bring themselves under control.

If the student is not acting out physically but continues to be verbally disruptive, and if attempts at within-classroom time-out have failed, it is time to find a way to remove the student from the class.

Once again, portray the intervention as a way to help him rather than as a punishment. Point out to him that you want to teach the class but currently you cannot, and therefore you are asking him to go somewhere so he can calm down. The first place you may try is the hallway. While other students are working on an assignment, ask him to step out to the hallway with you because you want to speak with him in private. Don't make it sound ominous. Instead, help him feel that, by stepping out of the room with you, he will avoid a discussion in front of other students that could be embarrassing.

While in the hallway, you can politely point out to him that he is behaving in a disruptive manner that prevents you from being able to get through the material you have to cover. If it is clear that he has calmed down quickly while talking with you in the hallway, allow him to return to the class and ask him to remain quiet while there. If he continues to be upset or agitated, ask him to go to the office or the nurse (which you will need to prearrange with staff) and tell him that, when he is calm, the nurse or the administrator will send him back (or advise him further).

If the student continues to be agitated and does not allow you to remove him without incident, you will need to call for help. While it will be very disruptive to the class to have the student removed from the classroom, it is nevertheless crucial to communicate to the student that if he continues to be disruptive, and does not respond to calm methods of getting him to stop or leave the classroom, you are willing to do whatever is necessary to remain in control of your class.

Most students attending regular-education schools will not require such a drastic measure. However, if a student is escalating beyond control—and especially if these episodes become common-place—her placement will need to be changed as quickly as possible, as it will be apparent that she is not able to remain in the regular class-room. Students in special education, especially those that attend pro-grams designed to address emotional and behavioral problems, are more likely to exhibit behaviors that require regular removal from class. However, teachers should not shy away from removing a stu-dent when she is behaving inappropriately and is not responding to less restrictive interventions. It is important to set limits and send a clear message to students regarding which behaviors are (and are not) permitted and what the consequences are for remaining disruptive.

In the Introduction, I provided an example of Mr. Spears and Traci, his ninth-grade student, a portion of which follows.

_____ **Example** _____

Mr. Spears asks the students to take out their homework assignments. Traci does not have hers. When he asks her why, she says, "Because I didn't feel like it. Social studies is boring."

"That's a zero!" the teacher says.

"I don't care!" Traci responds.

Mr. Spears attempts to go on with his class. However, Traci starts humming to herself. The teacher says, "Traci, please stop making noise."

Traci rolls her eyes but stops. A few moments later, however, she leans over to a classmate, and both start talking and giggling. The teacher says, "Stop that laughing and pay attention!" Traci ignores him and continues to talk and laugh.

Mr. Spears yells, "I said stop!" Traci says, "All right, all right." She becomes quiet for a few minutes. However, she takes out a magazine and starts reading it. Another student tells the teacher, "Mr. Spears, Traci is reading a magazine." The teacher, thinking that he must address this or risk losing control over his classroom, goes over to Traci and says, "What are you doing?"

(Continued)

(Continued)

"Nothing," Traci responds.

"Give me the magazine," the teacher says.

"No! It's not yours, you can't take it away from me," Traci says.

"But you can't read it in class," the teacher responds.

"OK, I'll put it away," Traci says.

Traci loudly shoves the magazine inside her desk and rolls her eyes, but she does not reengage in the class discussion. After a few moments, she starts to look out the window and loudly drums on her desk with a pencil. The teacher yells to her, "Stop that!" She again rolls her eyes but becomes quiet for a moment. She then yawns, stretches her arms, and loudly proclaims, "I'm bored," after which the class bursts into laughter.

Perceiving another challenge from Traci, the teacher yells, "If you don't knock it off, I will call your parents." Traci replies, "Go ahead. They're divorced. They don't care!"

• • •

This example illustrates an escalation within the classroom. Traci is exhibiting disruptive behavior that interferes with the teacher's ability to teach the students. As she continues to be disruptive, the teacher becomes increasingly agitated. Consequently, and most likely *because* he is getting agitated, the teacher does not take active measures to set limits. Instead, he tries to threaten, but this is ineffective. It is apparent that Traci is able to continue with these behaviors and does not experience any consequences for her inappropriate actions.

Instead, the teacher should communicate to Traci that she cannot remain within the classroom if she is going to continue to be disruptive. Here is an example of how this may be accomplished.

Example

Mr. Spears asks the students to take out their homework assignments. Traci does not have hers. The teacher does not confront her about it but indicates in his notes that she is missing today's assignment.

As the teacher proceeds with his lecture, Traci starts humming to herself. The teacher says, "Traci, please stop making noise."

Traci rolls her eyes but stops. A few moments later, however, she leans over to a classmate, and both start talking and giggling. The teacher says, "Please stop, because this is distracting others in class." Traci ignores him and continues to talk and laugh.

The teacher interrupts his lecture, tells the rest of the class to read the next page in the textbook silently, says, "Traci, please come with me for a moment," and steps out into the hallway. She follows him. While there, he says, "Traci, I know you want to talk to other students, but this does not allow me to go on with the lecture."

Traci responds, "But social studies is so boring!"

The teacher calmly responds, "Some find it interesting, some find it boring, but the bottom line is we have to cover the material in class. Would you like to go to the office for a while to compose yourself before you return to the classroom?"

Traci says, "No, I'm OK."

The teacher says, "OK, let's go back, but please be quiet, because if I cannot teach the class, I will have to ask you to leave."

Traci and her teacher return to class, and he resumes the lecture.

After a few moments, Traci starts to look out the window and loudly drums on her desk with a pencil. The teacher, while continuing to lecture, calmly approaches her and politely motions her to be quiet. She stops, and he acknowledges it by saying, "Thank you." Additional episodes of this type occur through the class, but each is handled in a similar manner.

● ● ●

This approach allows the teacher to set limits on what behaviors will be tolerated and remain in control of the class while avoiding conflict and confrontation. One brief time-out takes place that addresses the problem, at least momentarily, yet allows Traci to experience how disruptive behaviors within the classroom will be handled. Although this approach requires patience, and the teacher will need to work hard to control his frustration with Traci, this approach is more constructive, and over time, it makes at least some reduction in negative behaviors more likely. Of course, most of the time, the approach described in this chapter will not be sufficient to eliminate problem behaviors. Chapters 4 and 6 provide additional techniques that will help accomplish that goal.

• Putting It All Together •

The procedure described in this chapter will take some time and effort, but gradually you will see a decline in acting out. When appropriate, give your student a warning before utilizing time-out. Over time, the warning will be enough, and your student will learn that the warning is a signal to make a choice about what to do and what consequence will follow the wrong choice. However, do not use the warning with teenagers or for violent behavior. Your student must learn that violence will immediately result in a consequence.

As with the preceding steps, give yourself at least a week or two of practicing the time-out procedure. Don't continue with Step 4 until you feel comfortable using Steps 1–3 and your student gets used to the procedure so that each time-out episode is relatively short and calm. This may take some time, so be prepared to pause for a while before continuing with further parts of this program.

Step 3 Checklist

Learn How to Handle a Temper Tantrum

For violent acts, skip No. 1 and No. 2 under "Procedure," and take your student straight to the time-out location, as indicated in No. 3.

Procedure

1. Command
   - ❒ Tell your student to stop what he is doing.
   - ❒ Try not to yell, but speak loudly enough for him to hear and attend to you.
   - ❒ Maintain eye contact when possible.
   - ❒ Wait about 15 seconds.

2. Warning
   - ❒ Announce that if he doesn't stop, he will go to time-out.
   - ❒ As earlier, use a commanding tone and try to get eye contact.
   - ❒ Wait about 15 seconds.
   - ❒ Skip the warning when dealing with teenagers.

3. Take Your Student to the Time-Out Spot
   - ❒ Try to get your student to go on his own.
   - ❒ If necessary, assist him to get into the time-out spot.
   - ❒ Say, "Stay here until I say you can leave. You must be quiet."
   - ❒ Consider restraint if necessary (and permissible by law).
   - ❒ If your student doesn't stay, return him to the time-out spot and repeat as before. Repeat this as many times as necessary.
   - ❒ Once he is compliant with the time-out, start timing but *don't tell him how long you want him to stay there.* If you set a stopwatch, do so for yourself, not your student. Minimum sentence: two minutes (up to age five), or one minute per year of age thereafter.

❏ When using the technique with a teenager, ask the student to accompany you to the time-out spot and briefly remain there until calm. Do not make it appear as a punishment.

❏ If a teenager is agitated enough to possibly present danger of violence, briefly assess the danger by trying to calmly talk with the student, and if continued agitation and danger are apparent, obtain assistance as quickly as possible.

4. Release

❏ Go into the time-out spot and ask, "Do you know why I put you here?"

❏ Don't challenge your student into a confrontation; don't yell or lecture. Just get him to recognize the reason why you placed him in time-out. If necessary, just state the reason why he was placed in the time-out spot.

❏ Say, "Every time you do this again, I will put you in time-out."

❏ Return him to the classroom activities.

❏ Do not challenge a teenager into discussion about the time-out. When the student calms down, just allow him to return to the prior activity.

Step 3
Checklist

Create a Time-Out Spot

The time-out spot must be free of stimulation. It's best to use a place where your student can be isolated from other activities and students. Possible choices follow:

A corner of a classroom

A hallway or stairway

A nurse's office

The school's front office

The child study team office

Restraint Procedure

(Note: Make sure you have the legal right to restrain the student before attempting the following procedure.)

❏ Place your student in the time-out spot.

❏ Say, "Stay here until I say you can leave. You must be quiet."

❏ If she continues to physically act out, place your student in a standard chair and hold her from behind by the wrists.

❏ When restraining your student, be sure to stay out of her reach to prevent her from hitting, kicking, and biting.

❏ Repeat this to your student: "If you stop, I'll let go of your hands, but you have to sit here."

❏ When your student stops, let go of her hands but instruct her to stay in the chair. Be alert; she may start acting out again. If she does, quickly return to the wrist restraint.

❏ Don't be discouraged if you have to repeat this several times during initial implementation. Your student will need time to learn the rules of this procedure.

❏ The vast majority of teenagers do not need to be restrained. Instead, they should be removed into a safe environment where they pose no danger to themselves or others. This should only be attempted by properly trained personnel, not the classroom teacher.

Step 4

Construct a Behavioral Contract

Now that techniques for issuing commands and handling temper outbursts have been covered, you should be seeing an improvement and things in the classroom should be starting to go more smoothly. It is time to move forward and develop a powerful technique to address a wide range of behavioral problems.

Students' refusal to obey their teachers and lack of follow-through on academic tasks are among the most frequent complaints I hear from teachers. These problems cause tension between teachers and students on a regular basis. In fact, in some cases, teachers lower their expectations to avoid conflicts. In essence, these teachers give up and conclude that they simply can't get their students to do what they expect. There must be a better way.

Well, there is, and you will begin to learn to address these problems in this chapter. Essentially, you'll learn how to implement a system in your classroom where your student earns most privileges by performing tasks expected of him. This method is called a *behavioral contract*.

You may have tried some version of this procedure before and may have been unsuccessful. Don't give up. As with the time-out, there are many different ways of designing behavioral contracts. The way that is described in this book is effective with oppositional and defiant students, so read on and have faith—you *can* make it work.

The behavioral contract is absolutely crucial for you to administer. In my experience, it's one of the most effective ways to decrease management problems with your students, as confirmed by findings from my research with teachers and students (Kapalka, 2007b, 2008b). In addition, the contract becomes an important tool that will greatly assist you with the remaining steps in this program. Give yourself time to get this part of the program off the ground, and don't proceed further until you have it running smoothly. This step will probably take one to two weeks. Don't rush it; take your time. The better the contract, the easier it'll be to implement the remaining steps covered in this book.

What Is a Behavioral Contract?

A behavioral contract works on the principle of dispensing appropriate consequences following your students' behaviors—positive consequences after positive behaviors and negative consequences (or, at least, lack of positive consequences) after negative behaviors. In short, you'll reward the behaviors that are appropriate and punish those that are not. The moment I mention the term *reward*, many teachers object and tell me that I'm asking them to bribe their students—well, not exactly.

Rewards, Not Bribes

A philosophical distinction must be made between bribes and rewards. A bribe is something given to a person to entice her to perform a behavior that is improper. For example, politicians get bribed to support a specific position on an issue, company executives are bribed to perform special favors for individuals, and so on. As you can clearly see, these actions are wrong, and the recipients are paid, in effect, for selling out their principles and doing what they shouldn't do.

A reward, on the other hand, is a positive consequence one receives after performing a task that is proper and necessary but requires some time and effort. For example, capable students are rewarded with good grades, commendations, and certificates. A reward is a show of appreciation. A reward makes a person feel good and allows a person to feel a sense of accomplishment.

For some people, just the feeling of accomplishment is enough of a reward. However, it isn't realistic to expect this of many students. First of all, the ability to feel good just by conquering a difficult task mostly applies to adults, and very few children or adolescents are able to exhibit this kind of mature behavior. Second, oppositional and defiant students rarely want to perform a behavior that requires effort and time and that isn't fun. We must also remember that many of these students find academic tasks more difficult than other students, because they require focusing, impulse control, and frustration tolerance, skills that are difficult for oppositional and defiant students. To expect them to perform only to get a sense of accomplishment (or because it's the right thing to do) is simply unrealistic.

Even adults expect rewards on a daily basis. Would you go to your classroom every day if you didn't expect to be rewarded with a paycheck?—of course not. Just because you get paid for performing your job, does that mean that you are being bribed to do so? Again, it's obvious that the answer is no. In fact, if you carefully examine most of our day-to-day activities, you'll discover that most of what we do is because we expect to get some type of reward.

Most Rewards Are Free

Usually, when I first present to teachers the idea of rewarding their students, the teachers complain that they do not have the funds to buy anything for their students. Thus, they expect that I'm asking them to reward their students by buying things for them. This is a major misconception. Although a limited type of monetary reward (e.g., a small toy) can be included in a behavioral contract (I address this later), the basic contract is established with no monetary outlay of any kind. In other words, you wouldn't be buying things for your students as rewards—you'd use the rewards that are free and available to you every day. The idea is to implement an exchange in the classroom through which your students will earn privileges by performing certain behaviors.

Designing the Contract

An effective behavioral contract requires a thorough understanding of the behavioral principles that drive it, along with careful preparation. A contract is a tool that needs to be developed and personalized for each student so that it is effective. It is important to take your time and think through each phase carefully so that you develop a contract that is most likely to succeed.

Preparation

To start, you need to get a set of tokens that you will dispense to the student. The tokens that I found to be most effective are poker chips, easily obtained at your local five-and-dime or toy store. The chips are not expensive—just a few dollars for a box. Instead of poker chips, you can use other types of chips, including chips from some board games, even bingo markers, but poker chips really work well. They're large, so they're tangible and *feel* significant when held in your hand. It's also easy to keep track of how many you have, so they don't get lost easily.

With very young students, chips may not mean much because the child may have not sufficiently developed the concept of quantity. In addition, a child of three or four years of age may not be able to see any value in the chip, because he may not fully understand the idea of exchanging the chips for something more tangible. Instead, you may want to get a set of stickers and start a sticker book in which you will place stickers on a chart as he earns them. In fact, it helps to ask the parents of your student to go with him to the store and select a set that he really likes. Devote one page of the chart per day so that you can keep track of how many stickers your student earns each day.

With older students, especially those in middle school and high school, points work better than stickers or chips. You can establish a journal in which you write points as they are earned, or you can use slips that have point values on them (similar to Monopoly money) and give them out as the points are earned.

List of Responsibilities

Next, you need to make a list of duties that you want your student to perform. Start by writing down, for yourself only, the tasks that you want to have her do *every day*. It's important to start with only the things that you want done on a daily basis, not the responsibilities that occur once every few days or once a week. Those will be addressed later.

What responsibilities should you include? Well, that's entirely up to you. However, here are some suggestions. Start small, a maximum of about five or six items, and include only things that are part of your student's daily routine, such as handing in completed work after work time in the class, handing in homework (more about this in the next chapter), raising his hand before giving an answer, remaining in the seat throughout a specific period of time, and so forth. Each task on the list must call for a single, specific behavior. Define each behavior very precisely, so that there'll be no question in your student's mind as to exactly what it is that you want. To start, the responsibilities must be simple and easy to be checked and monitored.

Be sure to make your list appropriate for your student's age. A preschool-age child doesn't read yet, so if you work with this age group, you'll need to read each item on the list to your student every day. In addition, make the list very short, and make sure that your student can perform the tasks.

Once you've made your list, it's time to assign point, chip, or sticker values to each of the items. Start by assigning the value of one chip to the easiest item on the list, one that takes the least time and effort. Then compare the other items on the list to that one item and assign the other items the number of chips that are comparable with the time and effort that each task requires. In addition, assign higher chip values to items that your student is most reluctant to perform. Keep in mind what tasks have usually precipitated the most difficulties, and assign point values to these accordingly.

Take some time to talk with your student and explain that, starting on a specified day, you'll be implementing a new system in the classroom. Inform your student that there are some responsibilities that you want her to perform every day and that you'll show your appreciation by giving her some rewards. Your student will undoubtedly say, "What rewards?" At this point, it's best to ask your student to make a list of rewards that she'd like to earn, and write them down. Do *not* criticize your student for putting inappropriate rewards on the list. After all, your student may place it on the list, but that doesn't mean that you have to honor it. However, you need to make your student feel that she has input into this new program and that you'll at least consider what she wants.

List of Privileges/Rewards

Next, select from your student's list of rewards those items that you accept as appropriate and add additional rewards that you jointly discuss with him. Primarily include privileges as rewards. Examples include having recess time, selecting an activity (from a predetermined list) during recess, receiving a homework pass for one day (which can be specified for a specific subject only), being first in line when going to the playground or lunch, being allowed to leave the classroom to run an errand to the front office, and so forth. Some privileges that are utilized regularly throughout the day (e.g., time on the computer) may be best given out in shorter chunks of time; for example, time on the computer before and after lunch would be listed separately.

Your student will undoubtedly list some items on her list that require a monetary outlay. There are a few ways to handle this. One way is to include, as one of the rewards on the list, an item from a grab bag. One effective (and creative) way to do this is to ask the student's parents to take her to a toy store or a five-and-dime store and ask them to buy her 10 or 15 items that cost no more than about $2 each. Then, ask them to bring these to you, and you will put them in a bag and periodically allow your student the ability to earn a trip to that grab bag to select a toy from it. It's a good idea to allow only one grab bag reward per day and perhaps only one or two per week. It's also advisable to schedule those grab bag trips at the end of the school day so that she will not play with the item in school and instead will take it home with her.

As a way to include some of the more expensive items that your student wrote on her list (e.g., a video game cartridge), ask the student's parents whether they would be in agreement to allow your student to earn those items by being able to exchange a certain amount of points or chips she earns in school for a certain amount of money that the parents will set aside toward that item. If they agree (and, in my experience, most parents are eager to collaborate with teachers to bring difficult behaviors under control), you can make each chip worth a small amount of money such as a quarter, and the parents will allow your student to accumulate enough chips (as per the exchange rate) to be able to, in time, earn the item. Avoid recalculating exchange rates after you've implemented the contract. You don't want your student to lose confidence in the entire program and feel that you (and the parents) don't hold up your end of the agreement. Also, make sure that the reward you establish is one that the student's parents are comfortable with, and help the parents stand firm and only allow your student to earn those items that they are willing to give her.

When you figure out the exchange rate (i.e., the amount of chips your student earns in one day and the amount of chips he can spend), allow for some surplus. In other words, allow your student to earn about 15% to 25% more chips in one day (providing that he does everything on the list) than he would typically spend buying the daily privileges. This allows him to start accumulating chips for some of the bigger items.

As pointed out earlier, instead of chips, young students may respond better to stickers. For a specific number of stickers, allow your student a special privilege, such as being first to select a toy during play time or being first to choose a partner to play a game. With very young students, it is very important to keep the contract very simple and only focus on one (or two, maximum) behavior and consequence. In addition, the time frame must be adjusted so that the period of time during which you will monitor a behavior will be much shorter, and the reward earned by the sticker must be as immediate as possible.

A sample behavioral contract could look like the following.

Responsibility	Number of Chips
Completing assigned class work	1 chip per subject
Remaining on task during class work	1 chip per subject
Raising hand before giving an answer (per subject matter or per hour)	1 chip
Remaining quiet during class lecture (per subject matter or per hour)	1 chip
Remaining seated during class lecture (per subject matter or per hour)	1 chip

Reward	Number of Chips
Time on the computer (separately before and after lunch)	2 chips each
Being first in line for recess	4 chips
Being first in line for lunch	4 chips
Homework pass (limit of one per day)	10 chips
Trip to the grab bag	8 chips
Earning a $20 video game cartridge	75 chips

Starting the Contract

Pick a day when you want to start the program, and put it into effect at the start of school that morning. It's best to start on a Monday. It gives your student a sense of a fresh start at the beginning of a new week. Because this may be a new experience for your student, select a week that is relatively quiet and doesn't involve unusual events, such as extra stress because of annual tests.

Depending on the student's age, it is usually best to have your student keep her own chips. Each time she performs an item on the Responsibilities list, immediately give her the necessary chips. Likewise, each time she wants to do something that is on the Rewards list, she must give you the necessary chips to earn that activity. You may want to place a plastic bag in the student's desk where the chips will be stored. For very young students, establish a sticker book and keep it in the student's desk. Allow her to take it home every day to show her parents how many stickers she has earned. As she earns more stickers, she will be proud of her good behavior, and this will increase the effectiveness of the contract even further.

Once you start the program, follow through on every item on both lists. Each time your student performs the desired action, you *must* be watchful and give your student the amount of chips that were earned.

Don't forget to do this; your student will lose confidence if you don't keep your end of the agreement. Also, don't tell your student, "I'll give you the chip later." Do it immediately. Remember, as a teacher and a disciplinarian, you are most effective when you administer immediate consequences. A chip is a consequence, a positive one for a positive behavior. It will teach your student the most if it is given immediately.

Likewise, be consistent in requiring the chips from your student to cash in on the items on the Rewards list. Be ready to restrict your student's ability to do what's on that list, unless it is bought back with the chips. If your student protests and begins a temper tantrum, attend to the tantrum (as discussed in the previous chapter), but continue to follow through with the program.

Don't advance your student any chips that allow him to do something that he hasn't earned. When your student wants a privilege from the list but hasn't earned the chips, this presents a terrific opportunity for you to help your student learn that positive consequences—privileges—must be earned by positive behaviors. By sticking to this, you'll send a clear message to your student that you are serious about following through with this program. You'll also encourage your student to improve his ability to plan ahead and anticipate the consequences of his behaviors, a crucial component of self-control.

Sometimes your student may have spent all the chips early in the day and may not have an opportunity to earn any more chips for the remainder of the day. Or, perhaps the student had a bad morning and started to calm down in the afternoon, but earned very few chips thus far that day. In that case, you can do one of two things: You can stand firmly by the contract and restrict your student from doing anything on the Rewards list until the next morning, or you can give your student an extra (ad hoc) task for which she will earn some chips. If you do the latter, however, do so sparingly. Remember, you don't want your student to get the idea that you will accommodate her with other tasks so that she can earn the chips she needs to do what she wants. She needs to learn that she has to perform what's on the list or be restricted from what she wants to do. You must send that message to your student very clearly.

Sometimes I hear teachers lament that a student doesn't seem to care if he is restricted from an activity. These teachers feel that their students don't care about any consequence (positive or negative) they try to administer. This, however, is very misleading. When a student says, "I don't care" after he is restricted, teachers often take that too literally. Students do *not* like to be restricted. They *do* miss being able to do the things they want to do, but they don't want the teachers to know that these things matter. They want to communicate to the teachers that they control their own lives and make their own decisions.

Think about it: If your student lets you know that your restriction really got to him, he'd be admitting openly to you that you're in control. Instead, from his point of view, it's in his best interest not to admit to you that the consequence was, in fact, effective. By saying, "I don't care," he is trying to tell his teachers, "You can't get to me," even though the consequence probably did. So, don't listen to these statements. Remain consistent. After several times of being restricted, students usually realize that it's not fun being restricted and start to pay attention to the rules.

Who's in Charge?

It is very important to establish who will have the authority to monitor the responsibilities, give the chips, and exchange them for a privilege. First of all, only a teacher (and an aide, if one is in the classroom) is allowed to do this, and this establishes you as the one who controls the student's consequences. However, what about the student's other teachers? Step 7 addresses out-of-class situations and provides suggestions about ways to include other teachers in this program.

Which Classes Should Be Included?

When a child exhibits significant difficulties throughout the whole day, a realistic starting point must be established. Those classes in which the daily structure can immediately be increased will produce the most immediate changes in behavior. Usually, this means that the student's main classroom, where the majority of the academic instruction takes place, will be the initial target of the contract. Although problems may persist in other classes, gradual improvement (and increase in self-control) will take place even though some settings will not initially be included.

What about including lunch, recess, and other out-of-class settings? These settings have even less structure than any classroom; therefore, difficulties can be more likely. However, at this point, it is best not to include them. I address how to handle problems in these settings in Step 7.

What About Group Activities?

When students work in groups, problems are more likely to occur. In fact, this is such a common problem area that this book devotes another chapter to help teachers develop appropriate expectations and rules in group activities. It is OK to include certain expectations to be attained during group activities, but these should be very basic. For example, you can reasonably expect your student to keep her voice down, remain seated, and maintain attention on activities only within her own group. If you want to include these, it is best to make separate items in the Responsibilities list to clearly elucidate each of those expectations.

At times, you may want to develop a minicontract with a group as a whole, or with the whole classroom wherein groups compete with each other. For example, groups may strive to be the first to complete a project or be the quietest and on-task during a project, for which you reward with a prize (or an extra privilege) for the whole group. In such a situation, students in the group monitor each others' behaviors and remind each other about the rule(s) that everyone has to follow. In addition, you can privately tell a student (with whom you have an individual contract) that, if his group finishes first, he will receive extra chips from you for his added efforts.

What About the Reaction of the Other Students?

A contract between you and a student is a private matter. It is not necessary to disclose it to other students. Any discussion you have with a student about specific expectations, rewards, and so forth should occur privately between you and your student. However, sometimes other students may find out about it. For example, students may witness a sticker or a chip being dispensed or collected and ask about it. It is usually best to calmly redirect inquiries by pointing out to the inquiring student that you have different ways of working with different students, and it is a private matter between you and each student. If a student asks to have a similar system set up for him, you can certainly accommodate him and establish a rudimentary contract in which he earns something small (e.g., being first in line) in exchange for successfully performing some kind task or responsibility.

Teachers are often concerned that other students will become upset when they see a student being rewarded. In my experience, this fear is usually exaggerated. In the vast majority of cases, students may notice what is going on and have an initial reaction, but then they quickly learn that what the target student is earning is nothing more than what the other students get and that the target student must earn it while the other students get it pretty much automatically (e.g., time on the computer). In other cases, in which you do increase rewards for a student in comparison with others in the classroom, students will notice it but their reaction will depend on the extent to which the difference is dramatic. If the target student receives just a small degree of preferential treatment, such as being given more opportunities to run errands or be the first in line, the other students will have a reaction and may not initially like that you do that, but usually they accept it without major difficulties. In addition, if you establish a partial contract with the whole class (as discussed later), this problem will be resolved.

Often, it is beneficial to start a program, at least to a limited extent, with a whole class. Group activities are especially conducive to such a contract. Groups can compete to determine which one will be the quietest during an activity, which will complete the assignment first, which will get the highest grade (individually and on average), and so forth. You can also set up a contract in which students receive rewards for individual achievement (e.g., the highest grades, good behavior, etc.). This may help you structure the day for the whole class, so you may feel some relief because it'll help you organize your day.

As an example, you can set up a behavioral program for the whole class in which you will dispense chips or other tokens for good behavior ("gold slips"—premade slips of paper, each saying that this slip is given in appreciation of kindness or good behavior—are especially effective). Some of these can be given for standard, academic-type accomplishments, such as finishing the class work on time, obtaining the highest grade, or handing in homework for the whole week. In addition, these slips can also be given out for "random acts of kindness"—that is, in situations in which a student is seen using good self-control (e.g., avoiding an argument when being teased) or being kind to someone else (e.g., helping a student who exhibited particular difficulties or who dropped something).

The way in which these tokens can be exchanged for prizes or privileges can vary. Students who obtain at least a certain number of tokens for the week can earn a homework pass. One method used in some schools is to encourage students to accumulate these tokens over the whole marking period, and four times per year (or more frequently if desired) an exchange station can be set up with small prizes, books, and so forth that students can obtain with these tokens.

Using a system such as described here is very flexible and allows additional customization for a particular student. If the whole class is already following a program, a private arrangement can be made with a student to earn additional tokens for specific behaviors (as discussed in this chapter). All in all, a behavioral contract is an infinitely flexible technique only bound by the limits of your imagination.

Extending the Contract

The behavioral contract is a tool that is flexible and practical. It can be a skeletal, limited agreement that contains only one target behavior and a single specific reward or privilege. On the other hand, it can include a comprehensive list of behaviors—some of which occur daily and some of which are sporadic—and an equally complex system of rewards and privileges. Once the contract has successfully been in place for several weeks, various methods can be used to extend it to address a variety of additional problems.

The following suggestions are not meant to be implemented all at once. When you and your student are ready, you can extend the contract slowly, and always give your student approximately one to two weeks to get used to each new change.

Extending the List of Responsibilities

Thus far, the focus has been only on those tasks and behaviors that you expected daily. When you are ready, you may add those responsibilities that may need to be addressed more sporadically. These are discussed as follows, grouped by the type of approach that will work best for each type.

Sporadic and "Per-Need" Tasks

Per-need tasks are those that you want your student to perform on an ad hoc basis. These are tasks that come up infrequently and unpredictably; therefore, it is usually best not to write these items on the list (the contract). Instead, ask the student to perform these tasks as the need arises, and announce to the student what will be earned when the task is successfully completed. Make sure that the student understands exactly what you ask and knows beforehand what she'll earn by performing the task.

Sporadic tasks, in our definition, are different because they are not entirely unpredictable and yet they do not occur daily. Those tasks are best written into the contract. If the task is one that is usually performed on a specific day of the week (e.g., every Friday), specify the day in the contract when the task is to be done. Remember that one important goal of the contract is to help the student's day in school be more predictable for him. This helps him internalize your expectations, prepare appropriate responses, and anticipate consequences of his actions. As always, be clear with the description of the task and the specification of the reward or privilege.

Chunking

Instead of rewarding your student for each component of a routine, now you can give the reward only if the entire sequence is completed. For example, until now you may have given your student a separate chip for staying in her desk during a portion of the lesson and a separate one for remaining quiet. Now you can start chunking these tasks into a single entity, such as "perform appropriate behavior during class," and give a reward only when the whole chunk is complete. In this way, the routine becomes an all-or-none task, in which the reward is only earned after the entire routine is completed. However, be sure that the student is clear about which components make up the entire entity (in this example, which components define "appropriate behavior") and that you have obtained these components separately for some time. In other words, do not start chunking if the student is still having difficulty performing the individual behaviors on a regular basis. In addition, make sure that, even after you start chunking, all the components of that chunk are still clearly listed on the Responsibilities list so that your student has a point of reference that reminds her of exactly what it is that you expect.

Fading

With some tasks, you can gradually diminish and eventually discontinue (thus, fade) the use of the tangible rewards or privileges. All teachers want students to perform behaviors not only because they receive a reward, but also for other reasons (e.g., to experience the intrinsic reward of the behavior or to recognize that being cooperative and doing what is expected makes people respond positively, which makes a student feel good about herself). Impulsive, defiant, and oppositional students initially do not process situations long enough to consider those subtle consequences. For that reason, they must start acquiring a behavior through the use of more tangible, concrete rewards. Once the behavior has entered the internal repertoire, however, students can gradually shift focus from tangible rewards to subtle ones. In fact, it is those subtle rewards (e.g., receiving praise, positive feedback, and feeling good after you are successful) that will maintain the behavior long after the tangible rewards have been discontinued.

Before fading can be attempted, it is crucial to make sure that the student performs the target behavior so regularly that it is almost automatic (and so is the reward that comes afterward). Once that level of consistency is accomplished, you can now gradually begin to make it a little tougher for the student to get the rewards after the behaviors. In other words, gradually start cutting back by reducing the number of chips, points, or stickers that the behavior is worth. Go slow, and make sure to pause at each step in your cutting-back hierarchy for at least a week so that your student gets used to that level of reward. It is very important that you do not start to cut back too quickly.

First-Try Compliance

This procedure, popularized by Barkley (1997), involves giving your student an extra token if, when you ask him to do something, he does it immediately without your need to repeat the command. At first, announce to your student each time you will implement this procedure. For example, "I'm going to ask you to do something now, and if you do it immediately, I'll give you a chip." Then, ask him to perform some kind of a task. These tasks should be simple, direct, single-action items, such as putting something away or taking out a textbook. After you use this method several times with a heads-up, you can then inform your student that you won't remind him any-more about rewarding his compliance on the first try but that you *will* continue to reward him every time he immediately complies with your command. Be careful, however: Once you say this, you'll have to remember to reward the desired behavior when it happens or the procedure will lose its effect.

Over time, you can start to fade the continuous reinforcement and switch over to a more intermittent schedule (as discussed earlier). For example, tell your student that she'll earn five extra chips for each day during which she complied on the first try with at least 10 com-mands. In this manner, you'll gradually teach your student to be compliant without expecting a chip each time. Be careful, and don't progress to this last suggestion too quickly; your student may lose motivation to continue to try if your expectations are set too high. Praise your student each time she complies on the first try. Over time, you want her to become more compliant because she likes to hear your praise, not just because she'll earn extra chips.

Extending Rewards and Privileges

By now, your student may have started to accumulate some tokens. Sometimes, when a student has saved many chips, he may stop earning more and again start refusing to perform expected tasks on the list. Do *not* discontinue the contract. Continue to require your student to buy back privileges, and encourage him to spend the chips. As he spends more chips, the motivation to earn them will return.

Add More Rewards

Just as you expanded the list of responsibilities, it is important to expand the list of rewards. Discuss with the student's parents possi-ble items that your student may buy back with a larger amount of chips (e.g., toys, books, videotapes or DVDs, and CDs). Chances are, his parents may be planning to buy some of these things for him anyway, and you will simply provide a way for him to earn them. Likewise, go out of your way to entice your student to spend chips on extra activities that may come up. For example, during a class event or a forthcoming class trip, give your student opportunities to receive an additional reward (e.g., an extra snack) so that he can again experience how good it feels to earn rewards and privileges in exchange for good behavior.

Hoarding

If your student seems to be hoarding the chips and isn't buying back the privileges on the list (and refusing to perform many of the tasks on your Responsibilities list), your list of rewards and privileges may be too limited, and your student may still have enough free activities so that she is not motivated to follow the program. Make sure that your list is broad enough to include the common activities that your student likes and that she feels restricted unless she earns her privileges.

With a student who hoards chips and doesn't want to spend them, another technique may be useful. You can designate a "chip clean-out" week, during which he has to spend all of the chips that he has collected thus far. At the end of the week, the value of all of the remaining chips expires and the program begins from scratch. Performing this once in a while may be effective. Don't implement this too frequently, however, or your student will learn that saving chips is pointless, and this will diminish his motivation to earn the chips at all.

Token Costs

As you expand the contract, you may now start to punish your student by taking chips away for certain behaviors that you want to eliminate. To start this procedure, you'll need to make another list and label it *Costs* (not *Punishments*). A sample form is provided at the end of this chapter. Start by listing only one behavior that you want to punish. Common behaviors for which this works well include calling out, using bad language, acting aggressively, failing to remain seated, or talking during class lectures.

Be *very* specific, clear, and precise in defining what the behavior is and how much it will cost your student each time it happens. Make sure that it is a behavior that you will observe yourself. Don't rely on the reports of others, such as peers, to tell you that the behavior occurred. If you didn't see it or hear it, don't take the chips away.

Verbal outbursts that aren't severe enough for time-out are good candidates for initial chip costs. For example, if your student blurts out an obscenity when she is restricted, it can cost her five chips per episode. If your student goes into a brief verbal tirade, give only one punishment, even if several inappropriate things were said. However, if a minute or two later your student does it again, give her another chip punishment. If you use this suggestion, make sure to specify the phrases and words that you want to target. Don't be vague and just say "all curse words." This will only generate future squabbles about what is and isn't an obscenity. Instead, state exactly what you don't want to hear. Remember, the more predictable your student environment, the fewer management problems you'll experience.

Another candidate for chip costs is physical aggression. An outburst directed toward a teacher or resulting in classroom violence (e.g., throwing something) will immediately result in time-out (as discussed in Step 3). However, when you observe your student getting into an altercation with another student on the playground, as long as the amount of violence was limited (e.g., only pushing), a punishment with chip costs would be appropriate. When you set the chip costs, don't set them so high that one or two episodes of mild aggression (e.g., pushing a peer) will result in your student losing all of his chips. If that happens, what will you use when your student misbehaves again? After all, you have to be consistent. You can't advance chips to him that weren't earned, and you can't put a student into a "minus" account and take chips away later after they are earned. Be realistic and make sure that the punishment fits the crime.

Here is one final point about chip costs. At any given time, do not work with more than one or two behaviors for which you'll be taking chips away. Any more than that will result in confusion, and your student may begin to lose the chips too quickly, which may limit her motivation to continue with the program. After one problem has been eliminated (e.g., when your student stops using inappropriate language), you can move on to another problem that you want to address. Just make sure you wait for at least one to two weeks before making the switch so that you don't encourage the student to return to her old habits.

Using This Technique With Adolescents

With minor modifications, this technique is very effective with teenagers. As discussed before, it is best to use points instead of stickers.

Use a point sheet or a book to record all points that are being earned and spent. Point slips also work very well and operate in a system of exchange similar to money. Teenagers usually really like this approach, and it fits in with practicing the skills they are probably acquiring in their private life (e.g., learning money management).

Develop a discreet way of giving out and collecting the points. Teenagers usually feel very self-conscious about being the only student in class who follows this program, so it is important for teachers to be sensitive to that issue and respect their privacy. Usually, at the end of class, while students are getting ready to leave, teachers can take a minute or two to record points on the point sheet or give out the point slips.

Students in middle and high schools commonly attend several classes in a school day. This structure lends itself well to developing a few items that the student will work on during any specific period, and these items may be different from class to class or remain the same through the whole day. This affords the teachers much flexibility with selecting the target behaviors and specific classroom settings that will be included in the contract.

For adolescents, use age-appropriate rewards, such as increased time using the computer, the privilege to listen to an iPod (with headphones) at the end of a class, a homework pass, and so forth. A list of possible rewards is provided at the end of the chapter. Make sure each has a consistent value that you will expect every time. Also, for older adolescents, it may not be necessary to use tokens. Rather, you can use a one-to-one exchange for a privilege if a task is completed; for example, a teenager will be able to use the iPod only after he completed the assigned work for the day (and is at least 75% correct). Once again, be creative and remember that what seems small to you may be a big deal for your student.

Expanding the Contract

When it is time to expand the contract, you should start by extending the list of responsibilities and privileges. Sporadic and per-need tasks should be handled in about the same way. As with younger students, it is very important to be clear about the specific description of the tasks and the specific rewards that will be earned. Chunking is ideally suited for teenagers. Although younger students usually must start with discrete behaviors, many teenagers are able to start with displaying two or three target behaviors within a specific period of time, as long as those behaviors are clearly defined and you have realistic expectations about whether the student is truly able to perform these behaviors for the length of time that you expect. For example, requiring a temperamental, spirited, active teen to be quiet and sit in her desk for the entire class period is usually unrealistic. Instead, chunk the behaviors you want within a shorter period of time (e.g., "While we are working on this assignment, please be quiet and remain seated"). First-try compliance is also effective with teenage students, but a note of caution is again necessary. You should avoid appearing too bossy when you present the idea that listening when you first ask will result in a reward. Remember that teenagers struggle to control their environment. Instead, try to present the idea in a matter-of-fact manner. For example, "If you do this without needing a reminder, a reward will be given."

Be open to creative ideas about what teens may like to earn, even if some sound unconventional. Consider a one-on-one exchange—a specific reward after a specific behavior is performed (e.g., "If you finish this assignment in class before the bell rings, I will reduce your homework assignment for today").

Token Costs

As with younger students, token costs can be effective, but use them advisedly. Be very clear and specific, and try to plan ahead so that any points you take away do not exceed the points earned during the class. Similarly, avoid taking all of your student's saved points as a result of an incident. Instead, try to get as much mileage from the points as possible. Think small, and try to limit the amount of points you take away. Even small consequences, in the long run, will make at least some difference. On the other hand, if your student learns that a single episode of acting out will wipe out the results of all of his positive efforts, he will likely lose faith in the program.

Verbal outbursts are the most logical targets for point costs. Be sure to clearly define with painstaking specificity what you will punish, and remember that teenagers can be cunning and creative in finding ways of getting around your rules. Keep your cool and accept that you must give the teen some slack. Keep in mind that teenagers struggle to control their environment, including you, and you cannot make them stop just because you have rules and expectations. Set limits, but be realistic and choose your battles carefully.

——————• Putting It All Together •——————

Get the chips (or stickers), make the lists, and implement the contract. Be consistent and firm. Remember to give the chips each time a target behavior is performed, and collect the chips each time your student gets a target privilege or a reward. Immediate presentation (or collection) of the chips is one of the prerequisites for the contract's success.

If your student misbehaves but still performs the task on the list, give the reward anyway. Don't punish her by withdrawing the reward that she earned by performing the task. In other words, don't take away any chips during this step. Remember, you want to make your student's environment consistent and predictable so that she knows what to expect. For now, find another consequence for the transgression or use time-out (as discussed in the previous chapter), but allow her to use the chips she earned to get a privilege from the list.

In my experience, this component of the program is one that teachers often discontinue when the student's problems begin to diminish significantly. I understand why this is the case. Ongoing maintenance of the contract requires time and effort. As your student begins to perform regularly what's expected of him, continuing the exchange may no longer seem necessary. Whether it is a good idea to discontinue the contract depends on your student. Often, when the contract is discontinued, an oppositional student begins to gradually exhibit more problems. At first it may be sporadic, but over time, the problems may return to previous levels. With young students and those who are very impulsive and exhibit significant problems with self-control, it's best to continue to use the contract indefinitely, although it can be streamlined significantly. Consider some of the suggestions made in the latter part of Step 4, especially chunking.

Finally—please always remember to praise your student for performing each item on the list of responsibilities. Giving the reward isn't enough. Your student must hear that you like what he did and that you appreciate his sense of responsibility. Please refer to the examples of praise listed earlier in this chapter (and provided in a handout later).

Give yourself at least two weeks before proceeding to the next chapter.

Step 4 Checklist

Implement a Behavioral Contract

Procedure

1. Preparation
   - ☐ Get poker chips (or, for a very young student, stickers).
   - ☐ Start by making a list of responsibilities that you want your student to perform every school day. Initially, don't include weekly or sporadic tasks. Start small. The things that work best at first are things that involve a daily routine or schedule, such as
     - ○ Completing assigned class work
     - ○ Remaining on task during class work
     - ○ Raising hand before giving an answer (per subject matter or per hour)
     - ○ Remaining quiet during class lecture (per subject matter or per hour)
     - ○ Remaining seated during class lecture (per subject matter or per hour)
   - ☐ Don't include behaviors that you want your student to stop doing (e.g., arguing with others). To start, the responsibilities must be simple, clear, and easily checked and enforced.
   - ☐ Ask your student to make his own list of rewards. Don't criticize him for putting inappropriate things on the list. After all, you don't have to agree to what he wrote.
   - ☐ Use privileges as rewards. Examples follow:
     - ○ Having time on the computer (separately before and after lunch)
     - ○ Being first in line for recess
     - ○ Being first in line for lunch
     - ○ Receiving a homework pass (limit of one per day)
     - ○ Earning a trip to the grab bag
     - ○ Earning a $20 video game cartridge (chips will be saved over time)

☐ Include a grab bag of inexpensive items that your student can redeem, one at a time, with chips.

☐ When figuring out the exchange rate, make sure that she can earn a little more in a day than she can spend in a day.

2. Getting the Contract Started

☐ Usually, your student will keep his own chips.

☐ Your student will earn chips for performing certain duties and then use these chips to earn privileges (and small prizes).

☐ Only the teachers (or class aides) have the authority to give the chips and authorize the exchange of chips for a privilege or reward.

☐ If a student misbehaves but still performs the task, give the chip anyway. Find another consequence for the transgression. Don't take away a chip that she has just earned.

o During this step, do not punish by taking away chips. Use rewards only.

Step 4
Grid

List of Responsibilities

Name _____

Behavior	Amount

Step 4
Grid

List of Privileges/Rewards

Name _____

Privilege/Reward	Amount

Step 4
Grid

Token Costs

Name _____

Behavior	Amount

Step 5

Manage Transitions

Pause for a moment and review your progress. By now, you have implemented several important behavioral techniques, and your students should be exhibiting notable improvement. Behavioral problems should be diminishing, although it's normal to expect some day-to-day fluctuations. Like most of us, students also have good days and bad days; on some days, your students will seem more cooperative; on other days, they will seem more difficult. As with any other skill, self-control will not be the same from day to day. You probably experience days when it's harder to resist a fattening dessert or an expensive impulse item. Like adults, children and teens have days when their self-control varies.

Before attempting additional techniques, take stock and review how consistent you have been in using the previous steps. Do you remember to obtain eye contact *before* you issue a command? If this is difficult for you to remember and use consistently, please go back and review Step 1. Do you continue to argue after the command has been issued? If so, please go back and review Step 2. Does your student still exhibit frequent temper tantrums? Perhaps reviewing Step 3 will help.

Most important, how is the behavioral contract working? You and your student should now be coasting through most day-to-day classroom tasks. Some daily variation is expected, but your student should be generally more cooperative. If you're still experiencing problems in these areas, perhaps you should pause to review Step 4 before proceeding further. Are you consistent with giving your student chips or stickers each time he earns them? Are you consistent with charging for privileges and rewards? Is the contract designed with sufficient opportunity for success? Are you careful not to overuse the costs and punishments? A smooth-functioning behavioral contract is an important prerequisite for the success of the additional techniques covered in this book, so please take any extra time you need to improve the contract's implementation before you proceed to the additional steps.

A well-implemented behavioral contract is a powerful tool. It allows you the flexibility to add additional tasks, situations, and settings where you need to seek further improvement while maintaining opportunities for your student to receive immediate and tangible feedback after her behaviors. When used consistently over time, it allows your student to learn that appropriate behaviors result in positive consequences and that withdrawal of positive consequences (or sensible negative consequences) follow inappropriate behaviors. This gradually improves her ability to think before she acts and to evaluate her choice of option when deciding how to act in a given situation. For the remaining steps of the program, the contract you already established in Step 4 will be used to help you reduce three additional common problems that oppositional students often exhibit.

It was important for you to complete Steps 1 through 4 in order because each step built on the previous one and the skill mastered in each step increased the likelihood of success with the next step in the sequence. For the remaining techniques, however, proceeding in order is no longer important. Each of the following three steps addresses behaviors in specific situations and settings by adding these to the existing behavioral contract. This chapter focuses on reducing problems with transitions, Step 6 focuses on problems with interruptions, Step 7 addresses problems in common out-of-class settings (e.g., in the cafeteria or on the playground), and Step 8 discusses techniques to address problems with homework. Please feel free to complete these chapters in any order you choose, on the basis of your needs and those of your student.

The contract can be used to address a variety of problems. For instance, some students act out while transitioning from one activity (e.g., playing in the back of the classroom) to another (e.g., returning to his desk to do class work).

In the Introduction, an example was provided of several interactions between a second grader (Barry) and his teacher. A portion of that vignette is provided here.

_____ **Example** _____

As the recess comes to an end, the teacher asks the children to return to their assigned seats. Barry is the last one still in the back of the room. While the children return to their desks, Barry starts to build a tower with the building blocks.

The teacher yells across the classroom: "Barry, put those away and return to your seat."

Barry replies, "In a minute."

The teacher starts giving out a handout with a math assignment. Barry is still playing with the blocks. The teacher says, "Barry, I said put those away and come back to your desk."

"But I just want to finish building the tower!" Barry says.

The other children start working, and the teacher starts to circulate around the room to see if anyone needs help. Barry is still playing.

She raises her voice: "Barry, your work is waiting here for you." He responds, "I'm not finished!"

The teacher answers a question from another student and realizes that Barry is still in the back of the room. She tells Barry, "Come to your desk now, or I'll have to tell your mother you're not listening."

Barry does not respond. The teacher, still in the front of the room, answers another student's question and then yells, "Barry, did you hear me? I am calling your mother!"

Barry does not respond and continues to build.

The teacher, now visibly angry, marches toward Barry, starts to take the blocks out of his hands, and pulls him toward his desk. Barry starts yelling and crying: "But I was not finished! It's not fair!" He throws the blocks he still has in his hand across the room.

He gets to his desk, still crying, and his noise is disrupting the other students in the classroom.

_____ • • • _____

Why Are Transitions Difficult for Some Students?

Why do some students tend to have such difficulties stopping the current activity and transitioning into the next one? As with all behavior problems, there are many contributing factors, and understanding them can help teachers address those difficulties.

When a student is involved in one activity (e.g., playing), she may resist transitioning away from it to another (e.g., doing class work). One reason is obvious—she enjoys what she's doing and she doesn't want to stop. Consider a situation in which you, a normally functioning adult, are asked to interrupt an activity that you are enjoying. For example, you are watching an interesting television show, and someone approaches you and tells you that you have to stop. What is your reaction? You probably think to yourself, "No, I don't want to, I'm not finished." However, before you put these thoughts into words, you probably reason through the situation. You may think to yourself, "I don't want to, but it has to be done, so I guess I'll do it." Thus, before you select a response and decide what you will do, you reason through the situation, consider the consequences of various choices available to you, and only then select an appropriate response.

When faced with the need to transition, your student's initial (internal) response is the same as yours ("No, I don't want to, I'm having too much fun"). What he does next depends on his self-control. A student with good self-control will pause, think, and recognize that, "The teacher said it's time to return to class work, so even if I don't want to, I have to do it." However, an impulsive student with poor self-control has difficulty suppressing the external expression of his frustration. Thus, the internal reaction immediately becomes converted into an oppositional, verbal, and behavioral reaction to fight the transition.

Effective Technique to Reduce Problems With Transitions

How should you address problems with transitions? Here, I expand on a technique briefly mentioned by Barkley (2000) and extended and elaborated on in my own research (Kapalka, 2006). Essentially, it involves the application of several steps already discussed in previous chapters, particularly Steps 1 (giving commands), 2 (avoiding repetitions), and 4 (especially the "on-the-first-try" procedure).

As outlined in Step 5 Checklist at the end of this chapter, here are the components of a plan of action to address problems with transitions:

- Prepare yourself and your student.
- Set the rules.
- Set the reward for following the rules.

- Set the consequences for not following the rules.
- Give sufficient warnings.
- Implement the transition.
- Practice.

Let's review each of these components in more detail.

Prepare Yourself and Your Student

Teachers of oppositional students usually expect the worst. Because they have experienced so many problems in the past, they fear that each transition will result in similar problems. Consequently, teachers are usually on edge when they approach difficult students, and when they encounter resistance, the conflict escalates quickly. Eventually, the situation reaches an explosive point of no return. It is important to break this cycle. The teacher must remain in control and prevent the frustration from dictating the tone of the approach. Although it is difficult, the teacher must remain calm, which in turn will help the student remain calmer.

As with the other steps in this program, it is important that you set realistic expectations. Do not expect a student to *like* that you are requiring a transition. Accept that an oppositional student will protest, especially when you tell her to stop an activity that is enjoyable, such as play. Instead, expect some expression of displeasure and ignore it, as long as the student does not become abusive. It is important to keep in mind that you want to address the *behavior*, not the attitude behind it.

Set the Rules

It is necessary to establish appropriate structure before the transition is attempted. Follow the principles covered in Step 1, and set the rules for what needs to occur when the transition takes place. Be clear and specific. For example, "In a few minutes, we'll have to come back to your desk, so when I tell you, you'll have to do so."

You are preparing your student ahead of time so that when the transition comes, he is not caught off guard. A student with poor self-control becomes more upset when a change in activity or in expectations comes out of the blue (from his point of view). Without sufficient warning, his brain does not have a chance to prepare, so the oppositional reaction is likely to be much stronger. Instead, help him anticipate what is going to occur.

Set the Reward for Following the Rules

Tell your student clearly and specifically what she will earn for a successful transition. Because you now have a behavioral contract and you give points, chips, or stickers as a reward for good behavior, it will feel natural for you to offer a reward, such as, "If you turn off the computer and come back to your desk when I tell you, I'll give you two chips." Because your student has gotten used to the idea that good behaviors allow her to earn rewards, she'll easily recognize the value of trying hard to do so. With very young students, it may be better to use a more tangible reward, such as a sticker.

Set the Consequences for Not Following the Rules

Next, set the consequence for refusing or delaying the transition. Your student shouldn't get the reward that you previously announced. In many situations, this may be sufficient and is a natural consequence— if he doesn't earn something, he won't get it. Sometimes, however, it may be helpful to set a negative consequence for breaking the rules. The most appropriate negative consequences are those commensurate with the reward he would have earned had he followed the rules. For example, if he was promised that he'd earn two chips for turning off the computer when needed, he will lose two chips if he doesn't comply. Have him repeat the stated consequences to you: what he'll earn by transitioning appropriately, and what he'll lose by not doing so.

Give Sufficient Warnings

It's important to give your student these instructions ahead of the actual time of transition. This gives your student some time to prepare herself mentally. When a transition is expected, it makes it easier for her to exercise self-control, even if the transition is not desirable (e.g., when your student has to terminate an activity that she enjoys to return to class work).

Sufficient warnings must be provided. You may want to follow a "three-bells" approach. This is similar to what is used in theaters and at concerts during intermissions: One bell means that the audience must prepare to return to their seats, two bells mean that the show will begin soon, and three bells mean that the show is starting now. This works well when applied in the classroom. In this setting, the first bell occurs when the teacher sets the transition rule with the student. The second bell should be a warning, reminding the student that the transition is about to take place. It should occur a minute or two before the actual transition. The third bell signals the start of the actual transition.

Try to make the time frame of the transition's occurrence meaningful to your student. With a student who comfortably tells time, it's OK to have him look at the clock in the classroom when you announce that the transition will take place in, say, five minutes. Then, the second bell can come about two or three minutes later. With a younger student who doesn't yet have a sufficient concept of time lapse, giving a number of minutes is usually not meaningful. Instead, it's better to state a time frame that is meaningful from the student's point of view: If he's playing a video game, you can say, "When you finish this level, you'll have to turn off the computer." Of course, you'll have to have some idea beforehand when this may happen. Another suggestion is to use timers. Set a timer for five minutes and place it within your student's view. Then about midway through the period, come in and give him a reminder (the second bell). The third bell occurs when the timer goes off, and the transition must begin.

Implement the Transition

Once the rules and consequences are clearly set, implement the transition. Be firm but calm. Don't issue any more warnings. Transition your student immediately, regardless of her response. If she transitions successfully, administer the positive consequence and praise her for doing such a good job following your rules. If she doesn't transition as you asked, don't allow her to continue with the activity. Turn off the computer or pick up the toys. Don't yell or begin a conflict. Just inform her of the appropriate negative consequence as per the rules you set beforehand.

If he begins to have a tantrum, you may have to administer time-out, as described in Step 3. This underscores the need for you to be prepared for whatever responses you may get from your student. Again, allow enough time, and don't place yourself in a situation in which you feel rushed and can't do what you know is necessary to sufficiently address the situation. If a time-out is not immediately feasible, help your student along with the transition, even if he is crying and acting out. Most important, follow through with what you said would happen, and administer the negative consequence you previously set as soon as it is practical to do so.

Practice

As with the other techniques described in this book, it is necessary to practice this step as often as possible. The more opportunities you give your student to adjust to this new way in which you'll implement transitions, the more she'll become used to this technique and begin to comply. When you first begin this technique, practice several transitions per day, involving various situations. As your student becomes accustomed to this technique, she will begin to exhibit more self-control at transition times, and you'll note an improvement. Be consistent and give it time. The longer you use this technique, the more likely you are to see positive changes.

Here is how the earlier example may unfold when Barry's teacher follows the technique described in this chapter.

_____ **Example** _____

In about the last quarter of the recess period, the teacher quietly approaches Barry and looks where he is in his play activity. He is playing with the blocks and building a tower.

The teacher tells him, "Barry, please look at me."

She pauses until Barry looks at her.

"In a moment, we will have to start finishing up and get ready to return to our desk work. If you go back to your desk when I tell you to do so, I will put two stickers in your sticker book. Boy, will your mom be proud when she sees these! Now, please repeat what I just told you."

Barry repeats what the teacher says.

She responds, "Yes, good job. Please remember what I told you."

Because the teacher is still allowing Barry to continue, he is not likely to have a negative reaction, but he is now better prepared to stop the activity.

About a minute or two before the transition, Barry's teacher again quietly approaches Barry and states, "Barry, please look at me."

She pauses until Barry looks at her.

"We are just about ready to start our desk work, so finish your tower now. Take a handful of blocks to finish, and I will put the rest of them away. Remember, if you go back to your desk when I tell you, I will put two stickers in your book, and your mom will be so proud!"

The teacher removes most of the blocks away from Barry while letting him keep a few to finish his tower.

At transition time, the teacher once again approaches Barry and says, "Barry, please look at me."

She pauses until Barry looks at her.

"Remember what I said before? Please go to your desk right now. I will place two stickers in your book if you do so right away and I do not have to repeat it."

If Barry still has a block in his hand, the teacher waits a short while until he finishes the tower. If he still has a few blocks left lying around, she quietly removes them to reduce temptation.

As Barry gets to his seat, the teacher says, "Thank you for listening. I will put two stickers in your book as I promised before."

• • •

Using This Technique With Adolescents

The technique described in this chapter works well with teenagers. Here are some suggestions to make it especially effective with students in this age group.

Set Realistic Expectations

As mentioned before, keep in mind what is appropriate to expect given the student's age. Teenagers constantly test limits and attempt to exercise control over the outcomes of the situations in which they are involved. This is especially notable when teenagers are around other teens; thus, they feel that displaying their own will makes them appear cool and grown-up. Do not expect that teenagers will transition away from an enjoyable activity without commenting or showing their displeasure. Accept that it is not realistic to expect that these behaviors will cease entirely.

Instead, focus on the specific aspects of the behaviors that you seek. As suggested earlier, do not ask your student to *like* it; just ask him to *do* it. Even if he expresses some disapproval along the way, if he does what you ask, ignore the attitude and focus on the behavior. Of course, if the accompanying attitude breaks the rule of what is acceptable (e.g., the student calls you names or becomes violent in any way), immediately proceed with the suggestions covered in Step 3.

Set the Rules

As with younger students, seek attention and communicate the rule clearly and directly. It may be helpful to have the student repeat the rule you are establishing, but do not get into verbal sparring. If the student asks why, politely give a short explanation, but do not ask the student to agree. Express your appreciation for her efforts in transitioning successfully, even if she seems to exhibit reluctance or a negative attitude about doing it.

Set the Reward for Following the Rules

Try to think about a privilege that he is likely to value the most. If possible, set the reward to occur as immediately as possible after the transition. For example, give a good-behavior slip that he can use (perhaps, in conjunction with others, as per preestablished point values) before the end of the class period for earning five minutes at the end of the class to listen to his iPod (through the headphones), earn a homework pass, and so forth. Use your imagination, and talk to him about the choices of rewards. You will likely find that he will give you many ideas, some of which will be realistically attainable; if he participates in defining the positive consequences, he will be that much more likely to be motivated to earn them.

Set the Consequences for Not Following the Rules

As described earlier, it is best to use the withdrawal of a reward as the most natural negative consequence. In other words, she will not get whatever she would have earned. Most of the time, this is sufficient. Especially if the established reward was one that she was motivated to earn, its nonoccurrence will have enough impact to teach her that ignoring the rules does not result in a consequence that she desires.

If the student does not seem to care about the consequence, you may need to sit down with her and explain that enforcing successful transitions is really necessary for you to teach; communicate to her that in exchange for her efforts, you are willing to work with her to help her earn something that will be meaningful to her. Most of the time, when approached in such a manner, the teenager will work with you to determine a consequence that she will find meaningful and you will find realistic and attainable.

Implement the Transition

After the rules and consequences are clearly set, implement the transition. Remember to use the three-bells approach. Make bells one and two occur subtly, so that the entire class does not know that you are doing this for the benefit of a particular student. Announce them to all students. Once transition time has come, act swiftly and proceed with the transition without looking back—that is, without pausing to see whether the student likes the transition. Any hesitation on your part may be interpreted by him as a sign that you do not expect him to follow, which will only increase his tendency to resist. Instead, keep an eye on whether he is transitioning, but do not make it obvious to others.

Administer the Appropriate Consequence

If he transitions successfully, subtly give him the prearranged positive consequence (such as a behavior slip). You can do so by putting it on his desk while you casually walk by, or for even more privacy, placing it in an envelope that you simply drop off on his desk. Once again, it is helpful to ask the student how he would like you to give him what he earned. You will be surprised at some of the good ideas that he may have.

If he did not transition successfully, do not say anything; just move on with your lesson. Do not confront him or single him out in front of others. Simply withdraw the positive consequence he would have earned. If he asks for it, politely explain that he did not earn it and that soon he will have another opportunity to try again.

──────•Putting It All Together •──────

During transitions, students act out primarily because they find it hard to resist the impulse to continue with the present activity. When you set the rules and announce that a transition will take place, you are preparing your student's brain to process the change that is forthcoming. Remember to use a time frame that is meaningful to your student. Set positive and negative consequences for transitioning or resisting. The warning (the second bell) reinforces that the transition is near, further enhancing the value of the preparation. Then, implement the transition. Afterward, implement the appropriate consequence. As with all techniques in this book, practice as often as possible.

Step 5
Checklist

Address Problems With Transitions

Procedure

1. Set the Rules
   - ❐ About five minutes before the transition is to take place, warn your student that at a specific point you'll need him to perform a specific action.

2. Set the Reward for Following the Rules
   - ❐ Inform him of a reward he'll earn for successfully transitioning when needed.

3. Set the Consequences for Not Following the Rules
   - ❐ You may also set a negative consequence for not transitioning when needed.

4. Give Sufficient Warnings
   - ❐ About two minutes before the transition, issue a "second-bell" warning.

5. Implement the Transition
   - ❐ Provide an attentional cue (such as "Look at me").
   - ❐ Give the transition command. Remind your student of the reward for doing it immediately.
   - ❐ Look at him for 15 to 20 seconds after the transition command.
   - ❐ If your student is compliant on the first try, dispense reward and praise. If noncompliant, administer the consequences and proceed with the transition.

6. Practice
   - ❐ As with the procedure for interrupting, practice this technique as often as possible.

Step 6

Discourage Interruptions

If you've just completed the implementation of the technique described in the previous chapter—congratulations! You're well on your way through the program. By now, you should be seeing significant overall improvement in your students' behavior problems. In Step 5, you learned a method of expanding the use of the behavioral contract to address additional problems commonly encountered with in-classroom transitions. If you skipped the previous chapter, I encourage you to go back and read the first few paragraphs of that chapter before you proceed with the step described in this chapter. It's important to make sure that the behavioral contract you have implemented is working well and running smoothly.

A well-designed behavioral contract is a powerful and flexible behavior management tool. Not only does it allow teachers to address common problems with daily routines, but it can also be used to address more sporadic difficulties in specific settings and situations, such as interrupting while the teacher is trying to conduct a class lecture. This behavior is typical of very young students and generally improves with age. However, some students exhibit difficulties with interrupting that continue to be evident even after their classmates seem to have grown out of that phase. Consider the following example.

Example

Tommy is in second grade. He is sitting in the third desk in the middle row in his classroom. In the front of the classroom, the teacher is playing a Jeopardy-style game with the students about the basics of American geography. She is having the students take turns across each row and select questions that they wish to answer.

She starts with Maggie, the first student in the row closest to the window. Maggie selects a question for $100. The answer is, "These mountains are found in the state of New York." Just as Maggie is about to answer, Tommy raises his hand and calls out, "I know, it's the Appalachians!"

The teacher politely instructs Tommy to wait his turn and must now ask Maggie to select another question. Maggie does so and is able to respond correctly while Tommy remembers that he needs to wait his turn.

However, not even five minutes later, it is Kevin's turn. He sits in the first desk closest to the door. He selects a question for $200. The teacher reads the answer, "This is the longest river in the United States." Tommy again gets excited that he knows the answer and calls out, "I know, it's the Mississippi!"

The teacher tells Tommy that he is not correct and again asks him to wait his turn. She returns to Kevin, who correctly identifies the Missouri. The teacher, wanting to turn this into a learning opportunity for the class, asks a follow-up question. "OK, students, who can tell me the name of the second longest river in the United States?"

Tommy quickly realizes that the teacher has selected the very river he just named and blurts out, "That's the Mississippi!" without even raising his hand. In the excitement of the moment, and because he did not expect the question to be asked about the very river he just named, he forgot what the teacher asked him to do just a short while earlier (wait his turn).

The teacher again reminds him that he needs to stay quiet until she calls on him, and now the other students are also getting annoyed at Tommy and tell him to be quiet. He starts to get defensive and upset and sits back in his desk, visibly moping.

The teacher continues with the game. Because Tommy's feelings got hurt, he disconnects from the task for a while and two other students are able to take their turn. However, as the teacher is now beginning to work across the row of students where Tommy sits in the middle, Tommy re-engages and starts to show interest in the activity again.

The teacher asks Michael, the student who sits by the window in the third row, to select a question. He selects one for $300. The teacher says, "Remember, boys and girls, do not yell out your response even if you know it; just wait your turn." She reads the answer, "This is the largest of the North American Great Lakes." Because he was *just reminded to be quiet, Tommy controls himself and waits until Michael correctly identifies Lake Superior. The teacher, once again seeing an opportunity to extend the "teachable moment," turns to the class and says, "OK, boys and girls, who can tell me what country other than the United States borders Lake Superior?"*

Once again, because of the excitement of the moment, Tommy blurts out, "Canada!" Getting increasingly annoyed, the teacher once again tells Tommy to wait his turn, and once again the other students express their anger at Tommy by telling him to "shut up."

This pattern continues throughout the activity: When reminded, Tommy is able to control himself for a few moments, but every few minutes he forgets and blurts out responses again, forgetting that he must first raise his hand. Each time this happens, the teacher and the students get more annoyed, and Tommy's feelings get hurt. By the end of the activity, he has completely disconnected and is doodling on a piece of paper on his desk, no longer paying attention to the classroom activity.

●●●

Why Do Students Interrupt?

Why do some students outgrow this tendency rather quickly while others seem to continue to interrupt well into their middle childhood? The answer lies in the overall ability to use self-control. Students who tend to have continuing problems with impulse control into later childhood are likely to exhibit this tendency in many ways: poor judgment, frequent lying (usually in impulsive attempts to cover up acts that they think will get them into trouble), not being careful around traffic, and blurting things out when they think of them.

One of the ways in which students exhibit impulsivity is through calling out in the classroom. In the earlier example, Tommy is an impulsive student with poor self-control that likely causes a variety of behavioral problems, one of which is calling out in the classroom. In other words, Tommy is the kind of student whose teacher needs help to address behaviors that are difficult to control, and you may be reading this book because you are the teacher of a similarly impulsive student. I hope that what you are reading in this book is helpful to you in your quest to diminish those problems.

Sometimes it may seem that your student knows better but is still making the choice to interrupt and annoy. I recommend that you do not make such an assumption, as it tends to vilify your student. Instead, recognize that students exhibit this behavior in many situations. Impulsive students interrupt adults in various situations. The student's parents probably encounter this behavior all the time, and often this behavior may seem tolerable, even acceptable. In all likelihood, the student frequently approaches his parents and spontaneously says something that just came into his mind. When parents are not too busy (e.g., they are performing a common household task that can easily be interrupted), they may not notice that the child just interrupted them. However, when this occurs at an inconvenient and annoying time, such as in the classroom during a lecture or an activity, this same behavior is problematic. Keep in mind that impulsive students find it difficult to determine when it is OK to interrupt and when it is not.

Effective Techniques to Reduce Interruptions

As with other steps that you have implemented in the course of this program, it is important to follow a methodical approach that will help the student gradually bring the impulse to interrupt under control. Here, I present a sequence that will help the student clearly identify the behavior to be targeted, recognize the consequences for trying hard to control the impulse, recognize the consequences for not controlling the impulse, and practice the target situation repeatedly.

Now that you understand why students interrupt, how do you address this problem? I discuss here a technique briefly discussed by Barkley (2000) and significantly expanded and elaborated on in my research (Kapalka 2005c, 2005d) and practice. The principles and steps are similar to those that you used to address problems with in Step 5:

- Prepare yourself and your student.
- Set the rules.
- Set the reward for following the rules.
- Set the consequences for not following the rules.
- Practice the situation.
- Repeat the process.

Now I'll address each of these components in detail as it pertains to preventing interruptions. To illustrate the technique most clearly, I discuss methods to minimize calling out within the classroom. Other forms of interruptions can be addressed by adopting the same technique.

Prepare Yourself and Your Student

Before discussing specific instructions about addressing interruptions, I'll restate a few general principles. Never put your instructions in the form of a question. Always make them clear and specific (see Step 1). It's best to state your instructions before a situation occurs and remember the importance of eye contact (again, see Step 1). Stay calm and control your own level of anger and frustration.

Set the Rules

It's best to establish the structure necessary to address this problem well before you start the target activity. Select a day when you are ready to begin working on this problem. At the start of the school day, using the techniques outlined in Step 1, set the rules for what you expect of your student when you are teaching. Be clear and specific, and focus on a specific component of the school day, not on the entire day. For example, say, "When we do the multiplication flash cards today, instead of calling out your answers, you will have to raise your hand and wait to be called upon." You may want to ask your student to repeat to you what you just said.

It is best to start with only one or two specific and clear-cut activities during the school day when you will work on the calling out. It is important to recognize that it is not realistic to expect the student to control herself for the whole day. Rather, start with one or two half-hour periods in any one day, and as you gain more success with the technique, gradually expand it to include more of the school day.

Set the Reward for Following the Rules

Tell your student clearly and specifically what she will earn for following your rules. Because you now have a functional behavioral contract in which you give chips or stickers as rewards for good behavior, it will feel natural to offer a chip reward ("When you follow these rules and don't call out your answers while we are doing the flash cards, I'll give you two chips"). Your student has gotten used to the idea that good behaviors allow her to earn these rewards, so she'll easily recognize the value of trying hard to earn them. With very young students, it may be better to give a small, tangible reward, such as a sticker, immediately after the completion of the task. However, it's important to do so only after a clear, detailed, and realistic rule has been set. The reward should be given only after the student was successful in following the stated rule.

Set the Consequences for Not Following the Rules

First, your student won't get the reward that you previously indicated. In many situations, this should be sufficient and is a natural consequence for not following the rules. If she doesn't earn something, she won't get it. Sometimes, however, it may be helpful to set a negative consequence for breaking the rules. The most appropriate negative consequences are those that are commensurate with the reward your student was going to earn if the rules were followed. For example, if your student was promised that she would earn two chips for not calling out during flash cards, she will lose two chips if she calls out during the activity. Have your student repeat the stated consequences to you: what she'll earn by following the rules and what she'll lose by not following the rules.

Practice the Situation

Once the rules and consequences are clearly set, practice the target situation. Because you will probably set the rules in the morning and the target activity will take place a little later in the day, issue a brief but clear reminder to your student about the arrangement right before the activity begins. Remind her of the positive and negative consequences. Have her repeat these rules and consequences back to you. Then, begin the activity.

It is usually helpful, every few moments as you go through the activity, to remind all students that you appreciate how hard they are working on raising their hands and waiting to be called on before speaking. Although you are really saying this primarily to the one student with whom you have the arrangement, she will get the message, and you will save her the embarrassment of issuing reminders to her throughout the activity. Still, the fact that you again raise the issue will act as a reminder to her that she needs to continue to work on suppressing the impulse to call out.

Repeat the Process

It's very important to practice these target settings repeatedly. The first day you implement the procedure, practice it during at least one activity. As you progress, add another classroom activity every few days. The more opportunities you give your student to practice these situations, the more learning will take place. Don't be discouraged if your student interrupts the first few times you go through the activity. It may take a few tries before she is able to exercise enough self-control to suppress that urge. Obtain a baseline of at least four or five consecutive successes before you add another activity. Then, practice again until you obtain another baseline of success. This gradual increase can help you include most of the school day in just a few weeks.

Here is how the technique described in this chapter may be utilized to address Tommy's problems with interruptions.

Example

Tommy's teacher previously developed a behavioral contract with him in which he earns poker chips during each discrete section of the school day for remaining quiet and on task.

To address problems with interruptions, his teacher told him that another section will be added to his contract: He will earn zero, one, or two chips for raising his hand before he speaks during specified periods throughout the school day.

Today, the teacher is using flash cards. Before beginning that part of the class, the teacher discreetly approaches Tommy and reminds him that the next activity will require him to raise his hand before speaking and will count toward earning the extra chips.

The teacher continues on to that part of the class instruction. She stands close to Tommy to help him remain on guard and remember what is being worked on. Each time Tommy raises his hand before answering, the teacher winks at him or otherwise communicates to him that she is proud of him for the effort that he is making.

At times when Tommy begins to blurt out an answer, the teacher looks at him and raises her hand to remind him to raise his. As he does so, she tells him, "Good job!"

After the segment is over, she approaches Tommy and gives him a "thumbs-up" gesture to communicate that he has done a good job.

Using This Technique in Other Situations

The technique described herein is flexible and may be used to master other settings and problems with interruptions in other situations. For example, if you want your student to stop interrupting your face-to-face conversations with others, you can similarly create practice opportunities. Also, if you want to work on helping the student avoid interrupting peers while they are involved in activities, you can define the target activity in such a manner.

This technique is also useful in teaching students to remain on task (or, at least, at their desks) during an activity. Instead of targeting an interruption, target a time when students are expected to work independently on a task while sitting at their desks. As with the examples discussed earlier, set the rule, the consequences for following the rule, and the consequences for not following the rule; check the student's comprehension of the plan; and implement practice sessions. You will find that this technique lends itself well to a variety of situations in which you want to increase (or suppress) a specific behavior during a predetermined activity or period of time.

Using This Technique With Adolescents

Adolescents usually do not experience classic interrupting behaviors, such as calling out responses without being asked to speak. However, the technique described herein can be effective in addressing other issues that may be evident during a specific class or activity, such as having the student remain quietly at his desk while an activity is taking place or completing an assignment before a predetermined time has elapsed. This is a flexible technique that lends itself well to a variety of situations.

Set Realistic Expectations

As I advised earlier, keep in mind what is appropriate to expect given the age of the student. If the activity you are considering involves social interaction, remember that teenagers often feel self-conscious when around others and try hard to portray themselves as independent and able to make their own decisions. For example, when in the midst of a social activity, teenagers will make comments to each other and tease each other. You need to consider whether it is realistic for you to expect that none of these behaviors will take place. However, if the situation is one in which everyone is working quietly and no interaction is expected, the technique described in this chapter works well.

Set the Rules

As with younger students, seek eye contact (see Step 1) and communicate the rule clearly and directly. It is usually helpful to have the student repeat the rule you are establishing. If the student asks why, politely give a short explanation, but do not ask the student to agree that what you are requiring is a good idea. Express your appreciation for the student's efforts in obeying this rule, even if your student seems to exhibit a reluctant or negative attitude about it. Remember, you are not trying to get the student to like your rule. You just want your student to obey it.

Set the Reward for Following the Rules

As with Step 5, try to think about a privilege that the student is likely to value the most, and set the reward to occur as immediately as possible after the target activity. For example, if the student remained quiet during the work period, have the student earn some sort of privilege shortly afterward (e.g., listening to her iPod—with headphones—during the last five minutes of class). Use your imagination, and talk to your student about the choices of rewards. You will likely find that the student will give you many ideas, some of which will be realistically attainable. And, if the student participates in defining the positive consequences, the student will be that much more likely to be motivated to earn them.

Set the Consequences for Not Following the Rules

As described earlier, the withdrawal of a reward is the most natural negative consequence. Not receiving what would have been earned is sufficient most of the time. Especially if the established reward was one that the student was motivated to earn, its non-occurrence will have enough impact to teach the student that ignoring the rules does not result in a desired consequence.

If the student does not seem to care about the consequence, sit with your student and communicate to him that, in exchange for his efforts, you are willing to work with him to help him earn something that will be meaningful to him. Most of the time, when approached in such a manner, the teenager will work with you to determine a consequence that he finds meaningful and you find realistic and attainable.

Practice the Target Activity

After the rules and consequences are clearly set, implement the target activity. As with younger students, issue periodic reminders of the rules throughout the activity—for example, asking everyone to work quietly in their seats. Sometimes you can even issue a subtle reminder in the form of a lighthearted comment, such as a remark on how nice it feels to have a quiet period in the classroom to gather one's thoughts. Although you will not be speaking to the specific student, she will get the message and it will act as a reminder that helps her work toward getting the reward she wants.

Administer the Appropriate Consequence

If the target activity concluded successfully, express your appreciation to the whole class about how good it felt to have the activity go so well. When appropriate, issue the positive consequence. If the activity did not go well, do not single out the student and point out that he did not behave appropriately. Simply withhold the reward and try again tomorrow.

———• Putting It All Together •———

Students interrupt because it is hard for them to resist the impulse to say something whenever the thought comes into their minds. By implementing the technique outlined in this chapter, you are creating opportunities for your student to practice resisting this impulse. To help the student remain on track, select the situations in which interruptions occur most frequently and address them one at a time, practicing daily until you begin to note success and greater self-control. For each target activity, make sure to set the rule, the consequence for following the rule, and the consequence for not following the rule. Make sure your student understands. Administer the appropriate consequences after each time you practice the activity. Repeat this often. Remember, "practice makes perfect," so the more practice opportunities you give your student, the more success you'll experience.

As before, work on this technique for at least one to two weeks before proceeding on to other parts of this program.

Step 6
Checklist

Teach Your Students to Avoid Interrupting

Select target activities in which interruptions (e.g., calling out) are most likely to occur. Start with one activity and gradually add others only when the previous activities reveal consistent success.

Procedure

1. Set the Rules
   - ❐ On the day you begin the procedure, before starting the target activity, explain the rules to your student: He should not interrupt during the activity but raise his hand and wait to be called on before speaking.
   - ❐ Be clear and specific. The rule should not be "Don't misbehave," but "Don't interrupt; raise your hand and wait to be called on before speaking."

2. Set the Reward for Following the Rules
   - ❐ Tell your student clearly and specifically what he will earn for following your rules. One or two chips per activity works best.

3. Set the Consequences for Not Following the Rules
   - ❐ Do not give your student the reward.
   - ❐ Tell your student that if he does not follow the rules, he will not get the reward, and/or use a comparable chip cost.
   - ❐ Have your student repeat the rules, rewards, and consequences to you before proceeding.

4. Practice the Activities
   - ❐ At first, use short activities, such as a specific exercise or lecture.
   - ❐ Start small, especially with young students. At first, focus on only one activity.

❑ Issue periodic reminders *to the whole class* about the rule that everyone is following.

❑ If your student breaks the rule, do not single him out or point out his failure. Simply issue a reminder to the whole class. Afterward, calmly point out to him that he did not earn the reward today and that tomorrow you will try again.

❑ *If your student followed the rule, make sure to give praise and the promised reward.*

5. Repeat the Process

❑ Obtain a baseline of four or five successful trials of an activity before adding a second activity.

❑ Reward the student for each successful activity when implementing more than one.

❑ Gradually, with consistent success of the procedure, "chunk" the activities, if you prefer (as discussed in Step 4).

Step 7

Improve Behaviors in Out-of-Class Settings

By now you have implemented many techniques to address a variety of problems, and you should be noticing significant improvements in key areas throughout your typical school day. In the previous two chapters, I covered methods of expanding the use of the behavioral contract to address behavioral problems with transitions and interruptions. If you skipped the previous two chapters, I encourage you to go back and read the first few paragraphs of Step 5 before proceeding with Step 7. It's important to make sure that the behavioral contract you have implemented is working well and running smoothly.

A well-implemented behavioral contract helps you address common classroom problems, and it is also useful in addressing more sporadic difficulties in specific settings and situations. Through the use of consistent consequences, it gradually teaches students to think before they make choices of behavior. Over time, this becomes more automatic, and improvement is noted across the board.

Out-of-class settings often present a particular challenge. Consider the following example.

_____ **Example** _____

Darrel is a spirited fourth grader. He tends to talk too much in classes, and teachers have to remind him to stay on task. He is often described as a class clown. He likes to make jokes and gets a bad attitude when he is called on this behavior.

His behavior on the playground is especially difficult. He tries to play with the other children, but when they do not follow the rules he wants to impose on the play activity, he starts arguing, which quickly escalates to screaming and yelling, and sometimes he gets into physical altercations with other students.

The supervising teacher often has to intervene, but when approached about his behavior, Darrel usually says, "I wasn't doing anything!" and denies any wrongdoing. On a few occasions when he was caught engaging in some of these behaviors, he always insists that the other student started it and that he was not at fault.

Darrel's teachers have tried many approaches, including talking to him and asking him to "behave" and making him lose recess when he acts out. He has even received detentions for some of the episodes that turned physical. None of this seems to be making much difference and Darrel continues to have difficulties controlling his outbursts while on the playground.

● ● ●

Why Are Problems in Out-of-Class Settings So Common?

Outside of their classroom environment, students often exhibit more problems with self-control. The reasons for this are complex, but some factors are important to keep in mind.

First, a different setting does not follow the same patterns of behaviors and consequences that your student has become used to in your classroom, so he may be less likely to know what is expected. In addition, many out-of-class settings inherently have less structure. On the playground or in the cafeteria, there is less supervision and guidance. Your student may wonder, "What activities are allowed? How fast do I have to run before I get in trouble? How loud do I have to speak before I am told to quiet down?"

Another important contributor is the increased stimulation that students experience in low-structure settings. On the playground, kids are running all around, talking and bumping into each other. There are sounds and activities that grab attention, moment to moment, and therefore minimize the likelihood that students continue to think about self-control and good behavior. There are noises (and, in the cafeteria, smells) that divert attention and increase curiosity about what's happening. On the playground, many of the play activities involve a lot of physical activity. Put this all together, and students are likely to become overstimulated. When this occurs, the ability to utilize self-control is greatly diminished.

Effective Techniques to Address Problems in Out-of-Class Settings

The following suggestions are originally based on the ideas of Barkley (1997), upon which my own research has significantly expanded and elaborated, and their effectiveness in the current format is confirmed by my research (Kapalka, 2008a). Essentially, it involves the application of the approach outlined in Step 5, specifically adjusted to address problems in low-structure settings.

As outlined in Step 7 Checklist at the end of this chapter, here are the components of a plan of action that will help minimize problems and improve your student's self-control:

- Prepare yourself, your student, and any other staff involved in the target setting.
- Set the rules.
- Set the reward for following the rules.
- Set the consequences for not following the rules.
- Go into the target setting.
- Administer the appropriate consequence.

Each of these components is covered here in detail.

Prepare Yourself, Your Student, and Other Staff

Taking students to the playground or sending them to the library or the cafeteria requires preparation. First, it's important to consider what behaviors your student is likely to exhibit that will be most problematic. Think about previous problems that have occurred in that setting. Select those that were the most troublesome. This will help you focus on specific behaviors, an important component of success in these settings.

In addition, it will help you think realistically. Are you expecting a first grader not to run or yell on the playground or a teenager not to make comments during an assembly? That may not be possible. Always keep in mind what's realistic to expect of your student, given her age and personality.

If someone other than yourself will monitor your student's behavior, review the other steps that you have mastered thus far, including the importance of eye contact, the avoidance of repetitions, and so forth. Help the person who will monitor your student in the target setting establish appropriate expectations about the specific behaviors being monitored and the point at which the student is considered to have broken the rules. This consistency may be difficult to accomplish in some cases. All individuals have their own opinions and attitudes about what to expect. However, significant discrepancy in expectations will only contribute to the problems and will diminish the effectiveness of this technique. Do the best you can to get the other person on board with what you are trying to accomplish.

Set the Rules

Before going into the target setting, make sure that your student clearly knows what you expect. Focus on what it is that you want him to accomplish. This is best done right before the student goes into the target setting. Use the procedure described in Step 1, and obtain eye contact with your student.

Once you have his attention, set a few specific rules. The younger your student, the less you should expect. For example, a five-year-old can only follow one rule at a time, whereas a typical 10-year-old should be able to follow two or three rules. Explain to your student the rules that you want him to follow. The rules should be stated in a manner that is clear and sufficiently detailed so that you are leaving little to your student's interpretation. In other words, define exactly what it is that you expect. Don't say general things such as, "Be good" or "Don't misbehave"; this assumes that your student knows what you mean and what you expect, and this usually isn't true. Instead, be very specific: "Don't hit or throw," "Remain seated during assembly," and so on.

Tell your student that he'll get only one warning of the rules. Have him repeat these rules to you to make sure that he understands what you expect, including the fact that he'll get a single warning. Because the warning won't be repeated, it will be more meaningful. When a student hears a warning over and over, it becomes an empty threat and the student learns that it isn't likely to be administered. Instead, teach your student that he'll receive only one warning as a signal of an impending consequence.

If you will not be there to monitor your student's behavior, it is very important that you communicate with those who will be in charge of that setting. For example, communicate with the staff supervising the activities on the playground or in the cafeteria about the rules that you are setting and the program that you are implementing. It is important that the staff who will monitor your students follow your rules.

Set the Reward for Following the Rules

Tell your student clearly and specifically what she will earn for following the rules you stated. Again, be clear and detailed. A good example of a reward is earning five chips, stickers, or points (as per the contract you've already established). This underscores the need to have a well-functioning behavioral contract before attempting this step. If your student is used to the idea that good behaviors allow her to earn points (or stickers or chips) that can be exchanged for privileges and rewards, she'll easily recognize the value of trying hard to earn additional points.

Make sure you set a reward that is commensurate with the level of difficulty of self-control in the target setting. For example, your student should earn a greater reward for following the rules in a difficult setting (e.g., in a library) than on the playground. When setting rewards for out-of-class settings, it's helpful to set specific rules and rewards for each discrete setting, even if the rules and rewards will be identical. If other staff are involved (e.g., librarians), make sure that they have the same expectations of the student as you do. It's important to send your student a consistent message about what is acceptable and expected within a given setting.

Set the Consequences for Not Following the Rules

In many situations, it is sufficient that if your student doesn't follow the rules, he won't get the reward, and it is a natural consequence for not following the rules. Sometimes, however, it may be helpful to set a negative consequence for breaking the rules, especially if breaking the rules may result in significant adverse results (e.g., when the student may place himself or others in danger by his behavior). The most appropriate negative consequences are commensurate with the reward the student would have earned if the rules had been followed. If your student earns five chips for following the rules, he loses five chips for not following the rules. In some situations (e.g., places where following a rule may be especially difficult), this additional motivator may improve the likelihood of success and help your student try harder. Have your student repeat the stated consequences to you—what he'll earn by following the rules and what he'll lose by not following them.

Send Student Into the Target Setting

After the rules and consequences are clearly set, the student is ready to go into the target setting. Monitor her behavior to make sure that the rules are being obeyed. At first break of the rules or when your student is about to break them, warn her of the rules and the consequences. It's important that you give your student *only one* warning. If your student is able to follow the rules, point out how much you appreciate her ability to exercise good self-control and administer the positive consequence as soon as it's practical. Help your student feel a sense of accomplishment about her achievement.

Administer the Appropriate Consequence

If, after you issued the warning, your student breaks the rules again, inform him of the loss of reward or negative consequence and administer it as soon as it is practical. Try not to make it sound vengeful. You do not want your student to feel any worse than he already does. Instead, point out to him that he will have another opportunity in the future to try to succeed.

If he responds that he does not care, do not become engaged in an argument. It may be a desperate attempt on his part to save face. Instead, react calmly and simply reaffirm that the consequence will occur regardless of whether he cares.

What to Do if the Student Becomes Upset

Oppositional students, on learning that they have lost a reward or will receive some negative consequence, often become upset. It is important to attend to this situation immediately. If you see that your student is becoming angry and is beginning to get worked up, intervene right away. Pull her aside and attempt to calm her down. Try not to do this in front of others. Your student will likely become more upset if she gets embarrassed in front of other students. Instead, find a quiet, private spot and speak softly and calmly, even if your student doesn't do so. Remain composed and in control, and don't yell at your student; that will only upset her further. Ask your student whether she needs a minute or two to calm down. If you see that your student is too agitated to return, take a little more time.

If your student truly loses control and begins to have a tantrum, administer a time-out (see Step 3) immediately. Find an isolated spot where you can place your student to calm down. On the playground, pull the student aside or return to your classroom with the student. If the student was in a library or cafeteria, escort the student to the front office for a time-out. Treat it as a time-out and not a punishment that must result in further consequences. Unless the temper tantrum was severe, it is not necessary to immediately call the student's parents. Instead, allow the student to calm down, and give this procedure a chance to work.

Do not expect this procedure to work immediately. It will take a few trials; meanwhile, you may need to send the student to the office or administer another version of a time-out. It may not work immediately, but that does not mean that it will not work at all. As discussed in previous chapters, oppositional students usually require several trials before they learn from experience.

If you have given it enough time and the procedure is failing repeatedly, consider your rules. Are they unrealistic? Does the student get too overstimulated in the setting to regain control? Perhaps you need to implement some breaks midway to help the student calm down, or temporarily remove the student from the setting (e.g., arrange for the student to eat lunch in the front office for a few days) to give her a chance to get herself together before you rechallenge her with the same setting again.

Here is how the technique described in this chapter may be utilized to address Darrel's problems on the playground.

Example

Darrel's teacher previously developed a behavioral contract with him to help address some of his problem behaviors. Darrel earns points during each discrete section of the school day for remaining quiet and on task.

To address playground problems, his teacher pulled Darrel aside and stated that another section will be added to his daily point chart—0, 1, or 2 points for following these three rules on the playground:

1. He will not scream, yell, or curse.

2. He will not hit anyone.

3. He will not throw anything while on the playground.

(Continued)

(Continued)

Because his classroom teacher has preparation time while Darrel's class is on the playground, other teachers supervise the students. Consequently, Darrel's teacher arranged a brief meeting that included Darrel and the two teachers who alternately supervise students on the playground. During the meeting, Darrel and the teachers reviewed the rules and the points so that everyone had clear, consistent expectations.

Starting on a date that was mutually agreed upon by everyone involved, Darrel was asked to approach the teachers at the end of the playground period and get a slip of paper indicating the number of points that he earned during that day's recess. Those points are then added to the other points Darrel earns during the day.

If Darrel forgets to ask for the paper with the points, he receives no points, as if he earned 0 points for all three rules.

• • •

Using This Technique With Adolescents

The technique described in this chapter works well with teenagers. However, some modifications are needed to make it appropriate to this age group.

Set Realistic Expectations

As I advised earlier, keep in mind what is appropriate to expect given the age of the student. If the setting you are considering involves social interaction, accept that teenagers are concerned about acting cool in front of peers, and you cannot realistically set expectations that significantly counter these tendencies. For example, when in the cafeteria, teenagers need to remain socially active and tease each other, talk in an animated manner, change seats, and so forth. During an assembly, teenagers often need to make comments about (i.e., heckle) the presenters to look cool in front of their friends. You need to consider whether it is realistic for you to expect these behaviors to cease entirely.

Instead, focus on the specific aspects of these behaviors that are most troubling. For example, in the cafeteria, focus on yelling and throwing things rather than on teasing or changing seats. During an assembly, focus on their remaining seated. Think small. Do not try to fix all difficulties at once. Even if you are able to improve only a small aspect of the student's behavior, it is likely to be enough to make at least some noticeable improvement overall.

Set the Rules

As with younger students, seek their attention and communicate the rule clearly and directly. It is usually helpful to have the student repeat the rule you are establishing. If the student asks why, politely give a short explanation but do not ask the student to agree. Express your appreciation for the student's efforts in obeying this rule, even if he seems to exhibit a reluctant or negative attitude about it. Remember, you are not trying to get the student to like your rule; you want him to obey it.

Although older students, in theory, are able to process more than one item at a time, remember that you are likely asking your student to perform a behavior that, in her mind, is contrary to her expectations about what is appropriate in the given setting. For example, many students see nothing wrong with being disruptive during an assembly or being mischievous during lunch. Consequently, you will be more effective if you keep the rules you are setting to a minimum. Given everything that the student will likely be thinking about in the setting (e.g., how she presents herself to her friends), remembering just one rule is probably all you can expect under the circumstances.

Set the Reward for Following the Rules

Try to think about a privilege that the student is likely to value the most. If possible, set the reward to occur as immediately as possible after the target setting. For example, if the student receives a good-behavior slip at the end of the lunch period, have the student earn some sort of privilege right after lunch. For instance, the teacher of the next period could accept that slip as an excuse for a lateness of no more than five minutes to the next class. Perhaps when the student earns three good-behavior slips, he can exchange them for an extra treat during lunch the next day. Use your imagination, and talk to your student about the choices of rewards. You will likely find that the student will give you many ideas, some of which will be realistically attainable, and if the student participates in defining the positive consequences, he will be more likely to be motivated to earn them.

Set the Consequences for Not Following the Rules

As described earlier, it is best (and usually sufficient) to use the withdrawal of a reward as the most natural negative consequence: What the student would have earned, he has not. Especially if the established reward was one that the student was motivated to earn, its nonoccurrence will teach the student that ignoring the rules will not result in a desired consequence.

If the student does not seem to care about the consequence, you may need to get back to the proverbial drawing board. Once again, sit down with your student; explain that this rule is really necessary for you to enforce; and communicate to him that, in exchange for his efforts, you are willing to work with him in helping him earn something that will be meaningful to him. When approached in such a manner, the teenager will likely work with you to determine a consequence that he finds meaningful and you find realistic and attainable.

Send Student Into the Target Setting

After the rules and consequences are clearly set, the student is ready to go into the target setting. Because teenagers are in several settings throughout the day, it is very necessary for you to work with all the teachers and staff members that will be involved in monitoring your student's behavior and in administering any rewards and consequences. For example, reach out to the cafeteria staff to explain what rules you are establishing. Make sure to describe it in detail so that the staff in the setting with your student will have a similar idea about when the rule is being followed or broken. Stress that the student is to get one, and only one, warning. If earned, ask the cafeteria staffer to give the student a reward slip if the rule was followed that day. You may need to reach out to several staff people: Different individuals may work on different days, and you need to make sure that the program is followed as consistently as possible every day.

Administer the Appropriate Consequence

If your student returns to your class after the target setting, administer the appropriate consequence on the basis of whether the reward was earned. Similarly, if the consequences involve teachers whose classes the student attends after lunch, clear your ideas with them and ask for their participation and cooperation. Once again, make sure that you coordinate with them the specific consequences that will be extended and the circumstances under which the student will have earned them.

————• Putting It All Together •————

Preparing for out-of-class settings takes time and effort. Some teachers find it repetitive and tedious. However, it is necessary. Students who are impulsive and oppositional need frequent reminders (and motivators) to help them remain aware of the goals. The more frequent the reminders and the shorter the time segments in a setting, the greater the degree of progress. In the end, the improvement you will notice is well worth the time and effort.

As with other techniques discussed in this book, frequent practice is crucial. Using this procedure once does not guarantee that the student won't have problems again on the next trip to the same setting, but consistent use will likely result in diminishing problems over time. Use this technique with your student daily, perhaps once or twice per school day (for different out-of-class settings). Depending on the level of difficulties that you experience (and your student's age), you may need to start with just one rule and a relatively short duration in a setting, with frequent breaks. As your student begins to exhibit success, you can then gradually expand the time, and add additional rules to be followed. As before, work on this technique for at least one or two weeks before proceeding on to address other problems.

Step 7
Checklist

Manage Behaviors in Out-of-Class Settings

Procedure

1. Set the Rules
   - ❏ Before going into the target setting, get eye contact and explain to your student the rules that she must follow.
   - ❏ Set at least one, and no more than two or three, rules.
   - ❏ Be clear and specific. The rules should not be "Don't misbehave"; they should be very precise, such as "Don't run, hit, or throw," or "Remain seated while in the setting."

2. Set the Reward for Following the Rules
   - ❏ Tell your student clearly and specifically what she'll earn for following the rules. (Examples of rewards: five points or chips, a treat, a small prize, a "freebie" privilege)
   - ❏ Make sure you set a reward that is commensurate with the level of difficulty of the target setting. For example, your student should earn a greater reward for following the rules in a difficult setting (e.g., a library).
   - ❏ If possible, and if it is evident that the student cannot get through the whole time in the setting (e.g., during the whole lunch hour) without breaking the rules, break it up into segments and have your student earn a smaller reward during each segment.
   - ❏ When other staff members are involved, discuss the details of this procedure in advance, so your student will be exposed to similar expectations.

3. Set the Consequences for Not Following the Rules
   - ❏ Do not give your student the reward; or apply a specific penalty (e.g., loss of points or chips).

- ☐ Have your student repeat the rules, rewards, and consequences to you before going into the target setting.
- ☐ Send the student into the target setting.
- ☐ At first break of the rules, or when your student is about to break them, warn her of the consequences. *Only give her ONE warning!*

5. Administer the Appropriate Consequence
   - ☐ If she breaks the rules again, inform her of the loss of reward.
   - ☐ If she becomes uncontrollable, give her a time-out in whatever spot is reasonably available.

If your student follows the rules, make sure to give praise and rewards.

Step 8

Develop an Effective Homework Routine

Homework problems occur in many forms. Some students refuse to sit down and do homework. Others have problems staying on task and take several hours to complete assignments. Some students constantly ask for help and show little independence in doing their work. Others constantly forget their books, notebooks, and whatever else may be needed to complete the homework. Some students lie about whether work was assigned and constantly tell their parents that no homework was assigned by teachers when, in fact, homework *was* assigned and needs to be completed. Many students have a combination of these problems. In this chapter, I discuss methods of addressing all of them and how the behavioral contract plays an important role in improving homework-related problems.

Problems with homework are caused by various factors; some pertain to the school and classroom instruction, and others have to do with problems within the home. An effective strategy to address problems with homework, as confirmed by results of my research (Kapalka, 2007c), requires a combination of interventions, some of which need to be implemented within the classroom and others at home. In this chapter, both sets of interventions are discussed.

Because problems with homework require both teachers and parents to do some things differently, regular contact with parents is essential. Teachers usually meet with parents during predetermined times, such as parent-teacher conferences. However, this is insufficient for addressing the needs of students who exhibit more severe problems. In those cases, it is necessary to establish a regular pattern of communication between the teacher and the parents.

Parents are sometimes defensive when contacted by teachers. This is especially true with parents of oppositional and defiant students. Keep in mind that whatever problems you see within the classroom, the same student is even more likely to exhibit those difficulties at home. After years of dealing with a difficult child, many parents feel overwhelmed. Some even feel resigned. It is important that you recognize those dynamics before asking the student's parents to work with you in a collaborative approach. Be careful not to present yourself as a person who is blaming the parents for failing to teach the child better ways to behave. In such a scenario, parents are sure to react negatively and will not want to work with you. In addition, avoid appearing as if you are pressuring them to do more at home to "fix" your student's problems. Again, parents are not likely to react positively to such an approach. They already feel overwhelmed, and putting more pressure on them will not help.

Often, parents of difficult children are aware that they need help. When you contact them about problems with your student, make sure that they see your input as an attempt to help them develop some techniques that will likely result in improvement within the home as well as within the classroom. Then the parents will see you as someone who can help them, not just another person telling them they need to do more to get their child or adolescent under control. If they see you as someone with answers, they will more likely want to hear what you have to say.

Homework Setting

It's important for parents to set up a home environment that is most conducive to effective homework completion. To start, help the parents select a place in the home for the student to do homework. The place should be free from distractions and close enough so that a parent can monitor what the student is doing while there. The place should be quiet but not isolated. Examples of places that work well include the kitchen table (when parents are not preparing food), the dining room table, or a desk in the student's room, as long as it doesn't contain a substantial amount of distractions (e.g., a TV or video games).

The homework setting needs to be outside of the view (and sound) of the TV that other family members may be watching at the time, or parents should elect to turn off the TV. However, some students have more difficulties working in an environment that is too sterile and devoid of any stimulation. They may do better with a limited amount of activity around them. Sometimes it's a good idea to either allow the student to see the TV screen but turn the sound off or turn off the TV and turn on the radio in the homework spot. Encourage parents to experiment to learn what works best for their child or adolescent. In addition, the homework spot should be away from the telephone and any place where the student's siblings are playing.

Homework Time

When is the best time to do homework? This depends on each student's personality, the schedule and routine within the home, parents' preferences, and extracurricular activities that may determine when the student will actually be at home to do homework. Activities, sports, and club meetings all occur at different times, and the student's homework time needs to accommodate these schedules. However, as much as possible, your student should have the same homework time each day. The times that usually work best are about a half hour after the student gets home from school, about an hour before dinner, or immediately after dinner.

Doing homework immediately after school generally doesn't work well. When they get home, many students feel tired and need a little break before they start to do homework. Also, for many children, especially in early grades, the time right after school may be the only time when they can see their friends, so homework time should be set in such a way as to allow them to participate in at least some social activities. Whatever time of day is chosen for homework time, it's important that parents try to keep it consistent from day to day. One of the goals is to structure the student's day and make it more predictable. A routine that is repeated every day will eventually become internalized, and the student will learn to expect it.

Some specific times should be avoided. For example, it usually isn't a good idea to do homework right before bedtime. Late in the day, the mind is not as sharp and it is much harder to concentrate. Likewise, in the morning before students go to school is not recommended. Morning routine is usually rushed, and hurrying to do the homework while getting ready to leave the house on time prevents the student from being able to devote the kind of effort and energy required to learn from the assignments. Left on their own, however, students often choose these inappropriate times to do their homework. Parents should intervene and set a consistent time that is more suitable.

Also, if there are several school-age children in the home, it may be beneficial for the parents to set the same homework time for all of them. It will be easier for everyone to remember the same time, and parents will have an easier time monitoring their children and minimizing distractions. If a common homework time is established, parents need to make sure to separate each child into a different homework spot.

Begin a Homework Checklist or Journal

Establishing an effective means of regular, written communication between you and the parents is absolutely crucial for students of all ages. The best way to do so is to implement some type of daily written record of your child's assignments that you will check for accuracy at the end of each class or school day. Nowadays, most schools have adopted their own system of assisting their students in keeping track of homework. Some schools use homework journals or planners that are completed each day by either the teacher or the student. These usually resemble a notebook in which the work assignments are written. Sometimes, instead of a journal, teachers give each student a sheet at the beginning of the week that has spaces for homework in each subject to be recorded every day. This provides a convenient weekly record of all assignments in one place that can quickly be checked at a glance.

If your school doesn't have any of these in place, you can develop and implement one yourself. Get a blank, small notebook for your student in which you (or your student) will write the assignments each day. This procedure is particularly effective for younger students. For a student in fourth grade or higher, you can make up a variety of homework sheets that he can fill out (an example is provided at the end of this chapter). The sheets can be used either daily, in which case your student gets a blank sheet from you every day to fill out, or weekly, in which case he gets a sheet each Monday and uses it for the entire week. Either can work and each has its benefits and drawbacks.

The weekly sheet is more convenient, but some students may lose it in the course of the week. For many, the daily sheet works better, although it may be somewhat more cumbersome for the teacher (because you have to make sure that plenty of blanks are available and remember to give it to your student each morning), particularly if your student tends to be disorganized.

At first glance, this may seem to be an added chore for you, a busy teacher who is already attending to several different responsibilities each day. However, view this technique as an investment of time and effort that will pay dividends in the long run by helping your student learn to organize her work and keep track of her responsibilities. In addition, you probably already have attempted, unsuccessfully, many different ways to address this problem. This technique works well, and the effort is well worth the results.

Depending on your preference and the age of your student, you may fill out the journal or homework sheet yourself or ask your student to do so. If you prefer the latter, make sure that you sign or initial the journal or sheet at the end of each day; otherwise the entire procedure won't work. If your student has more than one teacher, each of you should check and sign the portion of the journal or homework sheet that pertains to your subject. All teachers should sign the form as the student is being dismissed from class. If there are no assignments given to the student that day, the entry must say "no homework," or something similar, and it must be endorsed by each teacher. This is very important—otherwise, the parents won't know whether the student is correct about having no homework or whether he simply didn't write it down. There is one more thing to remember: All entries in the journal or homework sheet must be made in nonerasable pen only.

Homework Rules

Once the setting and time are established at home, and the use of a homework journal or checklist has been arranged with your student and her parents, it's time to set the homework procedure. Your student must bring the journal or homework sheet home each day, together with all the work that is to be completed, including all handouts, books, and notebooks. Then, at the start of the homework time, the parents must ask her to show them the homework sheet completed for that particular day (signed or initialed by the teachers) and all the materials necessary to complete all of the work.

What should the parents do if the homework journal or checklist isn't signed, or if your student forgot a book or other item needed to complete the work? Any of these instances constitutes an incomplete homework preparation, and the consequence will be that your student doesn't earn a pass that day to buy back certain privileges established in the behavioral contract (this is discussed in more detail later in this chapter). Sometimes, parents drive the student back to school to get whatever he forgot. This is not a good idea, and you should advise parents against it. Help them understand that the student must learn to organize himself before he leaves school and to make sure that he has everything that he needs to bring home. Allowing him an "out" by bringing him back to get whatever he forgot will make it more difficult for him to learn that if he forgets something, no one will bail him out. This will encourage him to be more careful about—and put more effort into—organizing his materials before he leaves school.

Some students who truly are disorganized are not yet ready to be independent with packing their things at the end of the school day. You will need to plan to give them some assistance. Either teach your student that you will help her organize her things at the end of the day, or better yet, assign a homework buddy to work with the student. The latter intervention is particularly effective. It helps students improve their social skills, and it makes the helper feel good about being able to assist another student.

Doing the Homework

When the student is sitting down to do homework, parents should first help their child or adolescent organize the assignments by locating and categorizing, by subject, all work that has to be completed. This is best accomplished by reading each entry in the homework checklist or journal and grouping all needed materials (books, notes, handouts, etc.), by subject, on the homework surface where the work will be done (e.g., table, desk). Then, parents should ask the student which subject he would like to do first, and when that is selected, the parents should instruct the student to start working on the first assignment. When that assignment is done, the student should show his parents the completed work. Parents then need to check it briefly. The assignment is considered done when all of it is completed, most of it is correct, and it is legible. Parents should not get particularly picky about neatness. As long as the work is legible enough for you (the teacher) to accept it, it can be considered done. If it's really sloppy or if most of it is obviously incorrect, the student should be sent back to redo it. If he asks for help, parents should handle it in the way discussed later in this chapter.

When the first assignment is finished, parents should instruct their child or adolescent to start working on another one and to show it to them when it is complete. If a student is having particular problems with remaining on task during homework, it may help to reward him for each completed assignment (e.g., by giving him a chip, sticker, or another small reward). However, if parents do so, the reward should only be given if the assignment is finished correctly the first time, not if it has to be redone.

Earning an After-Homework Privilege

To teach the student that successful homework completion is rewarded by positive consequences, parents should restrict certain privileges until after homework time. For example, your student should not be allowed to watch TV or play video games until after homework is done. This means that the privilege should be restricted in the mornings and right after the student gets home. In other words, the student should be restricted from whatever privilege the parents select, from the time she wakes up in the morning until after she comes home from school and completes her homework. This approach increases her motivation to complete homework and teaches her that privileges are earned by taking care of one's responsibilities.

If the student forgot something on the list or if the list is not brought home, parents should not allow her to have the after-homework privilege that day. As you can see, this also serves as an added motivator for students who tend to procrastinate or take a very long time to do homework. After all, they'll be restricted from doing what they want until their homework is complete.

Providing Assistance

What if the student asks for assistance or says, "I can't do this assignment"? First, parents should monitor whether this happens on a regular basis. If it does, they should inform you so that you can consider the nature of this problem. It's possible that, for some reason, the student may not be learning an academic skill at an appropriate pace, and you may need to consider modifying the curriculum or assessing your student for possible learning problems.

When the student asks for assistance, parents should give it, but they should not complete the assignment for the student. They should just do a starter item or two with him and then have him complete the rest under their monitoring. If he refuses to try, they should tell him that he'll sit there until he decides to attempt the assignment. Remember, parents should send him back to do it again if it is done haphazardly.

Using This Technique With Adolescents

Principles described in this chapter are applicable for students of almost any age, including college-age students. However, for older students, some minor modifications are necessary. As students get older, their homework load increases and they need to gradually add studying to their daily homework routine. In addition, they gradually need to learn to be more independent and self-reliant.

Homework Setting

As discussed earlier in the chapter, the homework setting should be a quiet place, devoid of distractions, loud noises, siblings, and so forth. Teenagers need a more private place because they are likely to spend more time doing their work. Usually, a desk in the student's room works very well. As with younger children, parents should make sure that the student is not attempting to watch a TV program while trying to do her homework. Parents should also help create an environment conducive to doing homework, one that limits noise and distractions in the student's vicinity (e.g., keep siblings away). This is the time to make sure that the cell phone is off so that the student will not be able to send or receive phone calls, instant messages, and so forth. In other words, parents still need to ensure that the student is indeed working rather than getting involved in other activities.

Homework Time

Most teenagers are quite busy, participating in sports, clubs, and so forth. Consequently, it is necessary to be flexible with the homework time, and it may change from day to day, depending on the student's schedule. However, parents should not leave it all to the teenager to decide when he wants to do the work. On their own, many teens will choose to watch their favorite TV shows, chat with friends, browse the Internet—in other words, do everything *but* homework. Instead, parents should work out a schedule with their teen about when homework time will take place each day and monitor that this time is observed and that the teen is doing work, not just watching TV or texting his friends.

Teachers of high school students that have a long history of problems with completing their homework should consider establishing a study period in the student's schedule that will allow her to do her work. However, it is important to make sure that the study period is supervised by a teacher or an aide who will be able to help the student remain on task, organize her work, and answer any questions she may have. Many teachers find that this is the most consistent way of addressing problems with homework.

Performing homework in a study period allows the teacher another opportunity to provide consistent consequences. For example, if the student completes his work during a study period, the supervising teacher can note this in the student's homework journal, thus communicating to you (the teacher) that the student used the time in the study hall wisely. Consequently, this item can be incorporated into the contract and the student can earn additional points for making a good choice and completing his work.

Homework Journal

Many teenagers try to rely on their memory when an assignment is given to them, or they write the instructions somewhere in their notes and find that spot difficult to locate later. A homework journal is very beneficial for teenagers to use, although in my experience many teens resist the idea. Finding the right way to approach them is crucial.

Teenagers like to feel grown up. Thus, the homework journal can be presented to them as a tool that adults use on a regular basis. For example, when introducing the idea to a teenager, a teacher can point out that he uses a version of a homework journal every day—it is called a *calendar*. It serves the same function; it provides a space to record all the tasks we need to accomplish on any given day, and with it we can plan by consulting it for what is coming in the next few days and weeks. In fact, I have experienced many instances in which teens resisted a homework journal, but when given the choice, they obtained a calendar large enough to hold the homework data they needed to write down each day and seemed happy to use it. Be creative—find a way to help your student see it as a tool, a way to be more grown up.

Homework Privilege

Monitoring teenagers' compliance with homework is every bit as necessary as it is for younger students, but the way in which this is accomplished must be different. Instead of restricting a privilege that is earned daily and monitoring homework compliance every day, a weekly approach works very well for many teenagers.

Establish a weekly feedback sheet for teenagers that each teacher must complete. Many ways of accomplishing this are possible. Some high school teachers record all grades on the computer, so completing a printout at the end of the week is very easy. Others who are not quite so computerized may fill out a rubric that includes entries, per subject, for indications as to whether all homework was handed in this week and all tests and quizzes were passed (thus providing a way to monitor study habits, not just compliance with written work).

Help the student's parents recognize that leverage is necessary to encourage the student to be conscientious about studying and completing her homework. To provide such leverage, have the parents designate one weekend privilege that the student can only earn by showing evidence of having handed in all assigned work for the week and having passed (I recommend setting the minimum grade as a C or better) all tests and quizzes for the week.

Parents have many choices about which privileges to restrict. Some possibilities are being grounded for the weekend, having the car keys taken away, or missing special activities that occur during the weekend. I find that simply losing TV or video game privileges is not sufficient. It should be a weekend privilege with high reward value, one that the student looks forward to all week.

For example, if the privilege has to do with being off restriction for the weekend, a student starts out each week being grounded for the forthcoming weekend, unless he earns getting off the restriction. To do so, every Friday the student must go to each of his major teachers and receive a printout, or fill in a rubric, confirming whether all work was handed in and all tests and quizzes were passed. If all work was submitted and all tests were passed, the student earns weekend privileges. If the sheet or printout is missing, if it is incomplete (one of the subjects is blank), or if one of the teachers indicated a missing assignment or failed test or quiz, the student is grounded for the weekend.

Putting It All Together

This procedure, although seemingly complicated at first, is actually easy to administer. You will work with the student's parents to structure his homework routine and help him develop productive work habits. Gradually, he will internalize those rules. To help motivate him, he will be restricted from a privilege until after he completes his homework. If he forgets assignments or the journal or homework sheet, he will not earn that privilege for that day, and so he'll work harder to keep track of homework assignments in the future. This approach is effective in improving homework performance, but you'll need to help parents recognize that it takes a week or more to get this procedure off the ground. You and the student's parents should not give up. Stick to your guns, even if it means that the student won't watch TV for a week until he begins to bring home all that is required. Remember, if parents are administering proper consequences, they are sending a message to your student that homework is very important. As with the other steps, allow one to two weeks before expecting significant improvement.

Step 8
Checklist

Address Homework-Related Problems

Procedure

1. Homework Setting
   - ❏ Parents need to prepare a setting for the student that is free from distractions but isn't too quiet or isolated. Examples of homework spots that work best include the following: dining room table, desk in the student's room, kitchen table, and so forth.
   - ❏ The place needs to be quiet, away from view of family TV, beyond earshot of the telephone, and away from other activities.
   - ❏ It is sometimes helpful for the homework spot to have a minor stimulus present, such as a radio quietly set to a popular music station or a TV on but with the sound off.

2. Homework Time
   - ❏ Whenever possible, homework time should be consistent every day. The times that work best are about a half hour after the student comes in from school, about an hour before dinner, or immediately after dinner.
   - ❏ Homework time should not be set immediately before bedtime or in the morning before the student goes to school.
   - ❏ If there are several children in the home, it's helpful for all to have the same homework time.

3. Homework Checklist or Journal
   - ❏ Establish a homework journal or checklist with your student.
   - ❏ You or the student fill in the daily homework assignments, and you must check and initial each entry.

4. Homework Rules
   - ❏ If the student forgot the homework checklist, or if it isn't completed properly, he won't earn the after-homework privileges for that day (see item 6).
   - ❏ If the student brought home the checklist but is missing any of the assignments or the books necessary to do all of the work, he won't earn the after-homework privileges for that day.

5. Doing the Homework
   - ❏ At the start of homework time, the student must show his parents the homework checklist completed for that day.
   - ❏ Parents should help the student get organized at the start of the homework time to locate all the assignments listed on the checklist and the books necessary to complete them.
   - ❏ Parents should ask the student to do one assignment at a time and bring it to them to check when done. Then the student should start on the second assignment, and so on.

6. After-Homework Privileges
   - ❏ The student is restricted from exercising certain privileges (e.g., TV, video games, going out, seeing friends, phone time) until after homework is complete. It's usually best to pick just one or two of these.
   - ❏ After the homework is done and you've checked it, the student earns the after-homework privileges for that day.

7. Providing Assistance
   - ❏ Parents should give assistance only when the student asks or says that he doesn't know how to complete an assignment.
   - ❏ Parents should not do the work for the student. If assistance is needed, parents should do a starter item or two with him and then monitor the situation as he works on the remainder on his own.
   - ❏ Parents should check each completed assignment. If one was obviously done haphazardly (i.e., all or most of the items are clearly wrong) or if it is so unusually sloppy that it is barely legible, parents should ask the student to do it over before he proceeds on to the next assignment.

Step 8
Grid

Daily Homework

Name _____

Date _____

Subject	Assignment	Teacher's Initials

Conclusion

Maximize the Improvement With Additional Techniques

Congratulations on completing the program! Undoubtedly, it required dedication, patience, and perseverance. Along the way, you learned tools that help you address many behavioral problems in and out of the classroom. As you continue to use these techniques, you will likely experience further, gradual improvement in your student's overall manageability.

To maximize the benefit from the steps covered in this program, you may consider implementing additional techniques to help you maximize the positive changes you can expect from your students. These involve arranging your classroom and adjusting your teaching methods to establish an environment that is most conducive to effective behavior control. This final chapter will help you think through aspects of your physical space and your day-to-day classroom routine that can foster or hinder good behaviors. It is likely that you will not be able to implement all of the suggestions in this chapter. However, the more of these you put into practice, the easier it will become to manage the behaviors of all of your students. Please consider implementing as many as possible, given the dynamics of your classroom, your district's policies, and other limitations that you must observe.

Adjust Your Instructional Methods to Obtain Best Results

Some instructional techniques are more likely than others to stimulate interest and active participation. When students participate, they are less likely to exhibit behavioral problems; therefore, selecting instructional methods that hold the interest of all students is an important component of a comprehensive behavior management program.

Increase the Stimulation of Learning Modalities

Try to increase the stimulation of the predominant modality involved in your method of instruction. For example, many of the most common learning modalities, such as reading and writing, involve visual processing. There are many ways of increasing visual stimulation, but to understand these, we must briefly review how our eyes work. Processing achromatic stimuli (e.g., black letters on white paper) involves just one relatively small portion of our visual sensorium. Our eyes have rods and cones that are responsible for our vision. Without color, only the rods become stimulated, and the subsequent amount of perceptual stimulation is similarly small. When color is used, our cone cells become stimulated and the subsequent brain stimulation is more significant. In fact, the cones are prewired to respond proportionally to the intensity of the color—the more intense the color, the faster the cones fire and the higher the amount of cortical stimulation. The higher the amount of brain stimulation, the more difficult it becomes to divert your attention from that task.

Teachers can use this information to help stimulate the student's visual processing. Rather than using achromatic handouts and assignments, use as much color as possible, the more intense, the better. Content printed on colored paper, especially bright red, purple, or mustard yellow, draws the eye to it and increases the amount of time spent attending to that task.

This tip can be helpful when applied to other learning modalities as well. For example, when using auditory stimulation, such as when students take turns reading, make it more fun by having students act out what they read in some way or have them take turns in a group scenario in front of the class. This increases the intensity of the auditory stimulation and involves another stimulation, thus leading to the discussion of the benefit of simultaneously utilizing multiple learning modalities.

Use Multiple Modalities

Most of our instructional methods involve one dominant modality—for example, visual (when reading), auditory (when listening to the teacher lecture), or graphomotor (when writing). If one of those happens to be weaker for a student, he will more likely disengage during the activity that primarily involves that modality. However, avoiding that modality during daily instruction may not be possible. For that reason, it is beneficial to utilize instructional methods that involve multiple modalities. For example, verbal or expressive modality may be combined with visual modality when students read a passage and then complete an assignment in small groups that is based on what they just read. Also, the class can be divided into two halves and students can compete in a game that involves a physical task (e.g., being the first to get to the back of the room) and a successful answer to randomly selected questions that reinforce the learning; points can be given for both components. Many teachers find that adding a tactile component to common academic tasks, such as playing a game that involves movement or putting together a project, reinforces the other learning modalities and further engages students.

An excellent way of utilizing multiple modalities during learning is to use educational games on the computer. Because it is a game, most students—even teenagers—usually engage quickly in the task. In addition, computer programs and games commonly involve tactile, visual, and auditory modalities. So much of the brain becomes involved in processing the activity that little is left over for anything else (e.g., protesting or arguing). In addition, time on the computer can become an effective classroom privilege that a student can earn through good behavior (as discussed in Step 4 of this program).

Academic Assistance

Because you cannot utilize multiple-modality teaching all the time, there will be times when your assignment or classroom activity will target that weak modality. Make sure that you make it clear to your student how she can obtain assistance. This may seem obvious, but consider that your oppositional student may have been experiencing conflict with you for some time and likely perceives you as someone who easily gets annoyed at her; therefore, she may be reluctant to approach you for assistance. Go out of your way to communicate to her that, although you need to maintain rules, you are also there to help and you want to hear from her when you ask her to do anything that she finds hard to do.

One method of increasing the availability of assistance is to provide sufficient learning aides. These can take many forms. Some may be classroom resources that the student can use while working in your classroom (e.g., a dictionary or a spell-checker), and some may involve afterschool resources that a student may consult (with the help of his parents, if needed) while doing homework (e.g., a useful

Web site that relates to the homework assignment). The more the student recognizes that you are doing all you can do to help him, the better his attitude will be in class.

Novelty and Stimulation

Repetitive, rote-oriented tasks cause the brain to habituate very quickly, and the student becomes bored with the activity. Consequently, it is helpful to come up with novel activities and assignments. Be creative. Think about current events or interests that students of that age commonly have. Allow the student some input into customizing an assignment in a way that will meet your academic objectives on the one hand but stimulate some of her interest (and a sense of fun) on the other. Think outside the box. For example, if rap was around at the time of the Civil War, what would a rap song sound like (reflecting a theme that you can assign)? Reach for ideas that will have a current feel but contain the content that you need to cover.

Variety is also very important. Try not to overrely on one type of assignment or one modality. Unfortunately, most of the cookbook-style curricula that we follow in school districts do not contain sufficient variety, and they easily bore students, particularly those who are impulsive and oppositional. Those students crave stimulation and novelty. Think about how you can tap into those themes when you prepare lesson plans and assignments. Success in this area will greatly improve your student's engagement in the classroom, and in turn, his behavioral problems will significantly diminish.

Build Opportunities for Success

Impulsive, oppositional, defiant students commonly develop a negative expectation of their academic abilities. Their poor tolerance of frustration and a weak learning modality (e.g., problems with writing) affect their motivation because they recognize that they have to work hard to produce a product that is at least of acceptable quality. In addition, because they frequently argue with their teachers, those students usually conclude to themselves that the teachers do not like them; consequently, they do not want to work hard to satisfy the standards that those teachers impose on them.

Teachers should try to reverse this negative pattern. The way to do so is to stack the deck and think about classroom activities that the students can most likely perform well. If the student plays an instrument, have her play a piece of music that relates to the theme you are studying. If she likes sports, have her construct a game that all students can play that will reflect a certain theme. Although these specific examples may not work for you, you get the idea. It is necessary to go out of the way to conduct an activity in which the student in question can succeed. If she succeeds, she will start to feel better about herself and your class. With repeated experience of success, her motivation to try harder in your class will improve. As her motivation improves, so will her behavior.

Implement Techniques to Address Distractibility

When students are off-task or have disconnected from the ongoing classroom activity, they are more likely to exhibit problem behaviors. Students who become distracted often get involved in behaviors that disrupt the class and interfere with effective teaching and learning. For example, students may start a conversation with their neighbors and may become defensive when the teacher redirects them. Students may lose their place in the class activity and feel reprimanded when the teacher makes them realize that they are not following the classroom routine. They may be embarrassed in front of their peers and exhibit a combative reaction that can turn into a confrontation. Thus, effective student behavior management includes planning ahead to address problems with distractibility.

Signals and Cues

Developing attention-getters and teaching students to recognize them is an effective way to reduce distractibility. Essentially, students learn that certain words, phrases, or behaviors you perform signal them to stop what they are doing, look at you, and await your instructions. There are many ways of accomplishing this, and cues can be issued to a whole class or only a specific student.

Group Cues

Most teachers find it helpful to teach the whole class that certain behaviors on your part signal that they need to stop whatever they are doing, stay where they are, look at you, and await your further instructions. Common signals include flashing lights quickly two or three times or using a bell, buzzer, or other sound. At times, especially if the class seems very involved in an activity that involves movement or a significant amount of noise, it is helpful for the teacher to "freeze" and stand in place, perhaps raising one or two hands in the air. Although only a few students may recognize this at first, a few more will, and they will begin to pass down a chain-style message to other students to get them to stop whatever they are doing. Like a domino effect, students one by one respond to this cue and ease current activity. Even the most troubling student will also likely stop under pressure from peers. It may take a short while, but the whole class will quiet down and look at you, which is exactly what you were trying to accomplish.

Individual Cues

Although group cues are very effective when you need to summon the attention of your entire classroom, you can use individual cues to redirect a single student.

Individual cues fall into two broad categories, covert and overt, and each has its advantages and disadvantages. Covert cues do not interrupt the flow of the class activity you are directing, and with practice you can begin to weave them seamlessly into your teaching activities. They can be performed when you do almost anything, even lecture to your class. The most effective covert cues involve subtle body language that signals to a student that he needs to think about what he is doing and check whether he is doing what is expected of him (as opposed to daydreaming, talking to others, etc.). For example, let's say that you are doing a reading activity and students take turns reading a passage, but one student seems to be looking around, getting involved in another's business, and so forth. A subtle but effective way to bring him back on task is to simply start walking over toward him. If he is positioned so he is looking away from you, walk over so that you are in his field of vision, and do not say anything to him but start walking in his direction, while students simply carry on with the reading activity. When the teacher walks near, most students perform an automatic mental check about what they are doing and whether it is appropriate at the moment, and they adjust their behaviors accordingly.

Try not to turn this into a challenge or confrontation. You may want to start by not looking directly at the student. Look elsewhere (e.g., at whoever is reading out loud at the moment) but walk toward the off-task student. If you are getting very near and he is still not picking up on your presence, then look at him, but try not to say anything. You do not want to embarrass him or single him out, as this will make him feel bad and he will probably react defensively (or, at least, he will remember that you embarrassed him and become angry with you for being mean to him, which will affect his reactions to you in the future).

When your physical proximity is still insufficient to redirect him, use physical touch as an attention getter. Casually walk over toward him, do *not* look at him directly, and gently touch his hand or shoulder. If that is not enough and he seems puzzled as to why you just did that, silently point with your finger at what is on his desk (e.g., his reading book) to nonverbally indicate to him that you are directing him to get back on task. Because you do not look at him while doing so, he will feel less embarrassed, and the whole interaction will seem much more subtle. Because your approach is very understated, he is not likely to become oppositional, argumentative, or defensive. In fact, techniques that use subtle body language are effective across all ages of students, even with teenagers.

One problem with these techniques, however, is that students over time habituate to them, especially when you find yourself having to use them many times per day, and they begin to ignore those cues. This is where developing overt cues may be helpful.

Overt cues are clear, but because these are *individual* cues, they should only be known to the recipient. In other words, you need to develop a set of signals that you will subtly issue while the class is in session, and no one but the target student will know that you just issued an attention-getter. These are more difficult to get off the ground, and require some trial and error, but they can be an effective supplement to covert cues, especially when your student needs to be cued frequently.

Pull your student aside during a time when the two of you can talk privately. Gently point out to your student that there are times in the classroom when you become aware that she is not paying attention, and you do not want to embarrass her in front of others, but you want to know how you can give her a reminder that will be known only to her; thus, no one else will know, but it will help her refocus and get back on task. You can say something to the whole class that will seem general enough that no one will be the obvious target, but your target student will know that you said it because you are trying to help her refocus; for example, "It is so nice when you are all paying attention, because it helps other students learn."

This technique takes time to become effective, but your student will appreciate that you are doing something to help her save face in front of others, and she will be more motivated to work with you. Of course, it is best to use a combination of covert and overt cues, and you will likely find that the mix of the two types of attention-getters will begin to reduce the frequency of off-task behaviors.

Self-Monitoring

Self-monitoring is a technique that involves teaching a student to use a cue to perform his own mental check to become aware of what he is doing at the moment and whether that activity is the expected one that students should be performing at the time. It also involves the use of a cue, but less teacher intervention is necessary because the teacher does not necessarily need to issue the cues.

The easiest cue to use is something that you point to in a matter-of-fact manner while the class is going on, and no one but your target student will know that you have just issued a cue for him to self-monitor. For example, you can teach your student that when you say, "Oh, look at the time, we better continue so we can finish this and move on," you are subtly cuing him to self-monitor. If the student does not hear your cue, it will not work, so it is important that the student is at least looking in your direction while you say that, and you may want to be close to him when you do so to make sure he gets the message.

Training a student to associate an item that she regularly looks at in your room, such as the clock, gradually helps her internalize that association and perform self-monitoring even when you do not cue her to do so. At first, with your efforts, she will gradually learn that, when you mention the clock, it means that she has to think about what she is doing and get back on task, if needed. Gradually, that association will strengthen enough so that she will begin to think about what she is doing whenever she spontaneously looks at the clock, even though it was not precipitated by your cue.

Although self-monitoring is potentially a beneficial technique, it is often difficult to implement. First, students must be old enough to be able to self-monitor. Usually, this is attempted with children in fifth grade or above. In addition, a student's personality must be taken into consideration. Because this is a technique that requires the student to perform a mental check on his own, a student who is extremely combative or exhibits minimal effort to comply with classroom rules and routines usually will not want to bother trying this approach. However, a student who seems motivated to do well but is distractible and highly defensive when redirected may appreciate that you are giving him more opportunity to bring himself under control.

Structure Your Class to Minimize Behavioral Problems

How you teach and manage students is crucial in minimizing problem behaviors, but the framework within which you deliver instruction must not be ignored. Some classrooms seem to invite more difficulties, especially from impulsive students who have poor self-control. Understanding these issues and properly structuring the physical space, scheduling, and classroom rules and regulations will help you improve the behavior of your students.

Prepare the Classroom Space

Think about the following example.

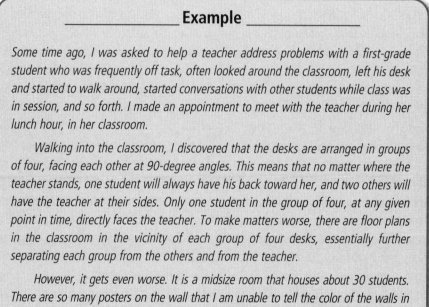

_____ **Example** _____

Some time ago, I was asked to help a teacher address problems with a first-grade student who was frequently off task, often looked around the classroom, left his desk and started to walk around, started conversations with other students while class was in session, and so forth. I made an appointment to meet with the teacher during her lunch hour, in her classroom.

Walking into the classroom, I discovered that the desks are arranged in groups of four, facing each other at 90-degree angles. This means that no matter where the teacher stands, one student will always have his back toward her, and two others will have the teacher at their sides. Only one student in the group of four, at any given point in time, directly faces the teacher. To make matters worse, there are floor plans in the classroom in the vicinity of each group of four desks, essentially further separating each group from the others and from the teacher.

However, it gets even worse. It is a midsize room that houses about 30 students. There are so many posters on the wall that I am unable to tell the color of the walls in the room. Even the windows have all kinds of stickers on them. Of course, all those wall posters and stickers are brightly colored, so the room has the appearance of an artist's studio with blotches of bright color scattered abundantly all around the room. Also, for good measure, there are things hanging from the ceiling: mobile-type decorations, a model of the solar system, and so forth, all brightly colored. As I sat down to meet with the teacher, I found myself being distracted and needing to refocus myself to pay attention to that teacher during our meeting, even though I am a middle-aged adult, and the meeting was held one-on-one. I can only imagine what this poor first grader, especially an impulsive one with poor self-control, must experience each day in this class.

_____ ●●● _____

This example exemplifies the things in a classroom setup that a teacher can correct to improve distractibility. Classrooms that encourage good attention and on-task behaviors have physical setups directly opposite of the classroom in the example. Instead of seating students in groups, students should sit in traditional rows, facing the teacher. There should be sufficient space between the desks to allow the teacher to walk between them, and increasing spacing makes it more difficult for students to become interested in what their neighbors are doing at their desks at any time. Although this desk arrangement is less convenient during group activities, it greatly enhances on-task behaviors at all other times in the classroom. Thus, the teacher has to pick the lesser of the two evils: Go through the minor inconvenience of rearranging the desks during small-group portions of the class, or deal with the negative consequences of a desk arrangement that makes all other times through the class day much more difficult.

Speaking of seating arrangements, the distractible student should be placed in a seat that is close to the teacher. As discussed earlier in the section that examined the use of cues, proximity affects attention. The closer the student is to you, the less likely she is to become distracted while you are teaching. If possible, seat the student away from sources of external stimulation, such as a window or a doorway. Additional sounds and images coming from such places will divert her attention away from you frequently during a typical class day. To further discourage distractibility, seat the student in such a way so that she is surrounded by students that do not like to be distracted and, therefore, will not go along with her attempts to start talking to them in the middle of class. At first, those neighbors may get a little annoyed that she is sitting next to them, but my experience is that, most of the time, this arrangement works well because the student learns that her neighbors do not like to be interrupted and therefore starts to use more self-control and suppress her impulse to bother them.

If you chose not to seat the student in the first row, seat her close enough to you so that you can walk toward her desk easily and effortlessly as you are teaching. Make sure that there are few obstacles between a place you usually stand and her desk, so that walking toward her and using the physical cues discussed earlier will be easy.

Teachers should be careful not to place additional distractions in the room. Keep posters to a minimum, and if you want to keep a specific one on the wall, try to seat the most distractible student so that the poster is behind him. Do not hang things from the ceiling, and do not place additional items on the floor between desks.

I am aware that some teachers will not like these "old-fashioned" recommendations. After all, the new approach to education is to make it more fun. However, once again, a teacher has to choose the option that ultimately will produce the greatest benefits with the least drawbacks and that ultimately will be in the best interest of all the students in the classroom.

Arrange Groups to Maximize Learning

You can take steps to have some of the remaining students in your classroom help those who are impulsive or distractible or have poor self-control. This is best accomplished by arranging study groups in which you assign students to work with each other on the basis of how they can help each other. Small groups of two to four students usually work best. Larger groups are not nearly as effective. Generally, the younger the student, the smaller the group should be, so in early grades, pairing works best.

When you select peers to work with the distractible, impulsive student, try to group her with those who are especially well-organized and motivated to learn. In this way, they will set limits on her tendencies to be off-task and will further help her during crucial points in the academic day, such as when she needs to get her homework assignments organized. In other words, pairing students who have academic needs with those who exhibit academic strengths is the best effective approach.

When I hold teacher training workshops, frequently I experience a negative reaction from teachers when I make the aforementioned recommendation. Teachers are often concerned that this arrangement is not fair to the academically "stronger" student who has to help the academically "weaker" student. However, these concerns are unfounded. Students who are motivated to learn, who have academic strengths, and who are less distractible derive a significant benefit from helping another student. Academically, because they use their existing knowledge and skills to help another student, it further reinforces the learning. Emotionally, they get the experience of how good it feels to help someone else, and they also enhance their self-esteem by being able to recognize that they have academic strengths that not every student exhibits. The student being helped also benefits. He is assisted by a peer, and most students are very receptive to peer assistance. It helps him build social skills as he experiences the limits that others place on him when he begins to act inappropriately. It also provides assistance to him when he really needs it, such as when he needs to organize his homework assignments. As the Dodo bird said in *Alice in Wonderland*, "Everybody wins."

Establish Classroom Routines That Are Conducive to Good Behavior

It is crucial to establish daily routines that promote good behavior. A few principles can be very helpful. First, think about the benefit of routines. They make the student's day more predictable, as she gradually learns what to expect. As she becomes better able to anticipate what will happen next, she is more able to prepare herself for it and, as a result, she will exhibit fewer problems. Students seem to exhibit most difficulties when they are told to do something that, at least from their point of view, comes out of the blue, and their brain therefore experiences a strong impulse to oppose. Expecting something to happen, however, prepares the brain, and even if what we are being asked is not necessarily to our liking, the reaction will be much less severe.

Scheduling

The easiest way to teach your student's brain what to expect is to try to train yourself to follow a consistent routine every day. To start, if you are the primary teacher and he spends most of his school day in your class, cover the academic subjects in the same order every day. Thus, he will learn to expect what happens next, and each transition will gradually become less problematic.

For each subject you teach, develop a consistent method of covering the material. For example, you may want to start with reviewing homework at the start of class, then proceed with a brief review of what you did yesterday, proceed on to activities that teach new material, and end with announcing (and writing on the board) the new homework assignments. If you regularly utilize several methods of teaching academic skills, try to get into a routine in which the student will be able to anticipate what you will do next. This technique works very well at all levels of education, including middle schools and high schools.

Structure

Teachers should keep certain things in mind with regard to structure. Activities that involve group interaction, movement, and so forth will usually precipitate more problems. I am not suggesting that you avoid using such teaching methods. To the contrary, they can be very effective in engaging and motivating an oppositional, impulsive student. However, teachers must accept that low-structured activity will precipitate more difficult behaviors, and therefore teachers must adjust their expectations about how the impulsive student will act. Teachers need to be careful not to set rules for these low-structured activities that are unrealistic and virtually assure that the student will get into trouble. In other words, some tolerance of minor misbehaviors will become necessary. In the end, this compromise is more than worth the benefits of using these teaching activities.

Conversely, activities that involve remaining at the desk should be very structured. Provide clear, detailed instructions about what needs to be done. Set a time limit on how much time students will have to complete any portion on their own. For older students, use the classroom clock to tell them when they are expected to complete their task. Cue them once about midway through to remind them about the time limit. For younger students, you may want to set a timer in plain view of all students and cue them once to look at the timer and see how much time is left. Large timers with big dials are suitable especially for that purpose. You will find that the more structure you are able to implement during desk work, the fewer difficulties you will experience with those portions of your school day.

Final Thoughts

As I pointed out at the beginning of this book, the techniques described herein are not quick fixes and require ongoing effort, perseverance, and time. I hope that you've seen firsthand that using these techniques helps your student become more manageable.

More important, as stressed throughout this book, using these techniques helps your students develop better self-control. Managing impulsive tendencies and developing the ability to stop and think before acting is a major developmental task. When mastered, it helps individuals become more successful adults. The strategies described in this book were designed to help you teach your students that important lesson through the consistent use of positive and negative consequences. Over time, you are assisting your students to learn to anticipate that positive behaviors meet with positive consequences and that negative behaviors meet with undesired ones. I hope that you feel a sense of accomplishment and pride. You are helping your students develop a skill that will likely make them well-adjusted adults.

References

Barkley, R. A. (1997). *Defiant children: A clinician's manual for assessment and parent training* (2nd ed.). New York: Guilford Press.

Barkley, R. A. (2000). *Taking charge of ADHD: The complete, authoritative guide for parents* (rev. ed.). New York: Guilford Press.

Barkley, R. A. (2006). *Attention deficit hyperactivity disorder: A handbook for diagnosis and treatment* (3rd ed.). New York: Guilford Press.

Barkley, R. A., Fischer, M., Edelbrock, C., & Smallish, L. (1991). The adolescent outcome of hyperactive children diagnosed by research criteria: III. Mother-child interactions, family conflicts, and maternal psychopathology. *Journal of Child Psychology and Psychiatry, 26,* 705–715.

Kapalka, G. M. (2001). *Longer eye contact improves ADHD children's compliance with teacher's commands—II.* Paper presented at the annual meeting of the American Psychological Association, San Francisco.

Kapalka, G. M. (2005a). Avoiding repetitions reduces ADHD children's management problems in the classroom. *Emotional and Behavioural Difficulties, 10*(4), 269–279.

Kapalka, G. M. (2005b). Longer eye contact improves ADHD children's compliance with teacher's commands. *Journal for the Advancement of Educational Research, 1,* 69–78.

Kapalka, G. M. (2005c). *Reducing ADHD children's problems with interrupting in school.* Paper presented at the annual meeting of the American Psychological Society, Los Angeles.

Kapalka, G. M. (2005d). *Reducing ADHD children's problems with interrupting in school—II.* Paper presented at the annual meeting of the American Psychological Association, Washington, DC.

Kapalka, G. M. (2006). *Reducing problems with transitions that young students with ADHD commonly exhibit.* New York: Association for Psychological Science.

Kapalka, G. M. (2007a). Avoiding repetitions reduces classroom behavior management problems for students with ADHD. *Journal for the Advancement of Educational Research, 3,* 15–22.

Kapalka, G. M. (2007b). *Efficacy of behavioral contracting with students with ADHD—II.* Paper presented at the annual meeting of the American Psychological Association, San Francisco.

Kapalka, G. M. (2007c). *Reducing ADHD children's problems with home work.* Paper presented at the annual meeting of the Association for Psychological Science, Washington, DC.

Kapalka, G. M. (2007d). *Parenting your out-of-control child: An effective, easy-to-use program for teaching self-control.* Oakland, CA: New Harbinger Publications.

Kapalka, G. M. (2008a). Managing students with ADHD in out-of-class settings. *Emotional and Behavioural Difficulties, 13,* 21–30.

Kapalka, G. M. (2008b). *Efficacy of behavioral contracting with students with ADHD.* Paper presented at the annual meeting of the American Psychological Association, Boston.

Kapalka, G. M., & Bryk, L. J. (2007). Two to four minute time out is sufficient for young boys with ADHD. *Early Childhood Services, 1*(3), 181–188.

Phelan, T. (2003). *1-2-3 magic: Effective discipline for children 2–12* (3rd ed). Glen Ellyn, IL: ParentMagic.